MARCO POLO

D0902765

SCOTLAND

SCOTLAND

NORWAY

Glasgow Edinburgh

DENMARK

IRELAND

Dublin

GREAT
BRITAIN

North Sea

NETHER-
LANDS

London

GERMANY

BELG.

LUX.

FRANCE

www.marco-polo.com

FREE!

THE TOURING APP

shows you the way...
including routes and offline maps!

GET MORE OUT OF YOUR MARCO POLO GUIDE

IT'S AS SIMPLE AS THIS

1 go.marco-polo.com/scot

2 download and discover

GO!

WORKS OFFLINE!

SYMBOLS

	Insider Tip
★	Highlight
●●●●	Best of ...
☆	Scenic view
☺	Responsible travel: for fair trade and ecology aspects
(*)	Telephone numbers that are not toll-free

PRICE CATEGORIES HOTELS

Expensive	over £120
Moderate	£75–120
Budget	under £75

The prices are for a double
room, for one night, with
breakfast

PRICE CATEGORIES RESTAURANTS

Expensive	over £30
Moderate	£15–30
Budget	under £15

The prices are for a three
course meal without drinks

CONTENTS

DID YOU KNOW?
Timeline → p. 14
Local specialities → p. 28
For bookworms and film buffs → p. 59
Bird droppings → p. 64
Budgeting → p. 117
Currency converter → p. 119
Weather in Edinburgh → p. 121

MAPS IN THE GUIDEBOOK
(128 A1) Page numbers and co-ordinates refer to the road atlas
(0) Site/address located off the map
(U A1) Refers to the street map of Edinburgh inside the back cover
Street map of Glasgow → p. 138/139
Coordinates are also given for places that are not marked on the road atlas.

PULL-OUT MAP
(🛺 A–B 2–3) Refers to the removable pull-out map
(🛺 a–b 2–3) Refers to the additional inset maps on the pull-out

INSIDE FRONT COVER:
The best Highlights

INSIDE BACK COVER:
Map of Edinburgh

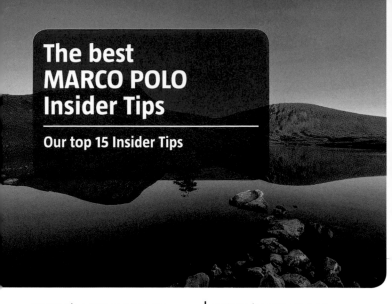

The best MARCO POLO Insider Tips

Our top 15 Insider Tips

INSIDER TIP Dundee meets Japan

The city on the Tay estuary boasts a timeless landmark: the new *Victoria & Albert* design museum is filigree Japanese architecture bordering on rustic highlands. In fact, the building marks the start of the new harbour front → **p. 72**

INSIDER TIP St Kilda the last outpost

All that remains today are the sheep, the seabirds and the wind. It's hard to imagine that people lived on these rough island crags for 2000 years. Today *St Kilda* is a Unesco World Heritage Site and a true paradise, especially for nature lovers and bird watchers → **p. 78**

INSIDER TIP Beach landing

It's a one-off worldwide: a runway that can only be used at low tide. On the Hebridean Isle of Barra the scheduled flight from Glasgow lands on the beach where shell seekers otherwise hunt for cockles in the mud → **p. 77**

INSIDER TIP Historic wrecks

There are seven sunken German battleships from World War I in the Scapa Flow, making it a popular site for experienced scuba divers → **p. 90**

INSIDER TIP Hitchcock-scenario

In the breeding season (May–July), the island of *Foula* resembles a scene straight out of Alfred Hitchcock's movie 'The Birds' with flocks of seabirds obscuring the sky → **p. 93**

INSIDER TIP Eye to eye with otters & other animals

Explore St Kilda archipelago by *sea kayak*: take a canoe tour with an experienced guide and let muscle power take you on an exploration of the unique wildlife along the west coast → **p. 107**

INSIDER TIP Sound of summer

Five days in celebration of the arts: every year at the summer solstice Orkney hosts the *St Magnus Festival* of classical music and dance, art and literature → **p. 112**

BEST OF ...

FOR FREE

● *Enjoy a smorgasbord extraordinaire*
Renowned paintings, a Royal Air Force Spitfire, stuffed giraffes, contemporary art: it is seldom that you will find such an entertaining mix under one roof. At Glasgow's *Kelvingrove Art Gallery & Museum* you get to see them all without even having to pay a penny → **p. 53**

● *Picnic in front of a Renaissance façade*
If you want to go inside the atmospheric ruins of *Caerlaverock Castle* there is an entrance fee. However, sitting on the lawns surrounding the fortress moat is free of charge and a picnic especially at dusk, with the ancient walls a special hue, can be ever so romantic → **p. 38**

● *Mull in sound*
Since Felix Mendelssohn-Bartholdy visited Mull and Staffa in 1829, the islands have a sound. You can listen at the *Mendelssohn on Mull* Festival in July. The concerts are free → **p. 83**

● *Chapel at the end of the world*
Homesick and seeking solace: this is what prompted Italian prisoners of war to build the *Italian Chapel* in the barrel vault of an old barn on the remote Orkney Islands during World War Two. This symbol of peace and reconciliation still moves visitors to this day → **p. 87**

● *Enigmatic stones*
Sunrise over the *Callanish Standing Stones* (photo) on the Isle of Lewis will catapult you back nearly 5000 years. Made of Lewisian gneiss, the sensation of standing solitary among them at the dawn of a new day is priceless → **p. 77**

● *Haunting cemeteries*
Admire the colossal collection of tombstones of important citizens in Glasgow's necropolis. And let the story of 19th century body snatchers, Burke and Hare, make the hairs stand up on your arms in Edinburgh's sombre *Greyfriars Cemetery* with accounts of how they dug up fresh corpses and sold them to the university's school of anatomy. → **p. 45, 54**

ONLY IN SCOTLAND
Unique experience

● *Edinburgh's majestic mile*
Everything that's typically Scottish is concentrated here. Along the *Royal Mile* in Edinburgh, you will find all things Scottish – go back to the Middle Ages with the strains of the bagpipe, ghost walks and quaint pubs → **p. 47**

● *Nessie mania*
Every year a submarine dives into Loch Ness to catch a sign of life of Scotland's most infamous legend: so far, without a trace. Perhaps, you'll discover something about *Urquhart Castle* → **p. 70**

● *Explore for miles on foot*
150 km/93 mi on foot from Glasgow to Fort William? Why not. After every day hiking along the *West Highland Way*, you can put your feet up in a pub. Outlaw Rob Roy once hid in the idyllic wooded eastern shore of Loch Lomond → **p. 71**

● *A whisky pilgrimage*
Only the Scottish could succeed in harnessing the spirit and taste of their country in a bottle! For connoisseurs there is the *Malt Whisky Trail* and you get to taste your way through the distilleries sip by sip → **p. 75**

● *Border collies*
Watch how these smart dogs are guided by whistles and calls as they shepherd sheep around a course. A visit to *Leault Farm* is not only great for the kids → **p. 111**

● *Royal Highland Games*
To see men in skirts tossing the caber or country dancing you should visit one of Scotland's many folk festivals. The guys are absolute pros! If you attend the main one in Braemar you could even get a glimpse of the Queen and her family → **p. 24, 113**

● *Folk music to get you going*
Celtic folk music is both melancholic and haunting and yet also very danceable. *Sandy Bell's* is an Edinburgh pub where it is played and sung at jam sessions – also at the Orkney and Shetland festivals (photo) → **p. 50, 112**

ONLY IN

BEST OF ...

● *Celtic pub stop*
The Ceilidh Place, a café-style restaurant in Ullapool, has a great bookstore and such a homely atmosphere that you won't mind whiling away some time until the sun comes out → **p. 84**

● *Rune graffiti*
The Vikings sought refuge in *Maes Howe* on Orkney and left behind intriguing runes that they carved into the chamber walls: interesting enough to take your mind off the rain (photo) → **p. 88**

● *They bite even in rainy weather*
Fly fishing on the River Tweed and in the Highlands is wonderful, even in wet weather. Wearing waders in the water, you cannot get any wetter. Guides instruct you about how to use the right bait for prolonged rainy spells. → **p. 37**

● *Gothic Revival architecture*
A pristine white Carrara marble chapel, a bedchamber with a ceiling with constellations and planets, an entrance hall like a church ... *Mount Stuart House* on the Isle of Bute is the epitome of Scottish neo-Gothic design and perfect for a rainy day → **p. 58**

● *Romantic times under the turf*
What can be cosier than watching the storms and lashing rains from the comforts of a luxuriously furnished cottage with expansive panoramic windows? Book into the turf-roofed *Blue Reef Cottages* that nestle into the hillside on the dramatic Harris coast → **p. 79**

● *Fun science*
Travel to the stars or to the intriguing world of Alice in Wonderland, observe cockroaches in captivity or be turned into a giant. The exhibits, Imax cinema and tower at the *Glasgow Science Centre* will provide lots of entertainment → **p. 53**

RAIN

RELAX AND CHILL OUT
Take it easy and spoil yourself

● *Heavenly repose*
Wake up well rested in a four-poster bed, spend unhurried hours in front of the fireplace, enjoy the view of the Highlands from your wing chair with a glass of wine in hand – *Darroch Learg Hotel* is just one of many Scottish manor houses and castles offering stylish relaxation → **p. 63**

● *Unwind at a city spa*
The *Sheraton Grand Hotel* spa in Edinburgh is a good place for hours of relaxation with its Turkish bath, saunas and variety of treatments not to mention a huge rooftop swimming pool → **p. 50**

● *In the mood for an Ayurvedic massage?*
Treat yourself to this rejuvenating four-handed Ayurvedic massage which is par for the course at the award-winning spa at the *Gleneagles Golf Resort*. Here, you can enjoy the whole repertoire of wellness treatments that range from a crystal steam bath to a hot stone massage in elegant surrounds characterised by wood, leather and luxurious fabrics → **p. 72**

● *Twilight hours in Edinburgh*
Head up *Calton Hill* at twilight to Edinburgh's own Athenian acropolis, which offers one of the most magnificent views of the capital city. Lean against one of the pillars, relax and enjoy the view and don't forget to take along sundowners → **p. 44**

● *Far from the madding crowd*
Want to get away from it all? Do as David Bowie and Leonhard Cohen have done in the past and visit *Holy Island* where you are invited to re-energise in its spiritual centre and Buddhist retreat. The mandala garden is lovely → **p. 58**

● *A Garden of Ede*
Of all of Scotland's gardens the *Inverewe Gardens* (photo) at Ullapool in the far north has to be the most stunning. Enjoy this sub-tropical paradise that is so very unusual for this part of the world → **p. 85**

INTRODUCTION

DISCOVER SCOTLAND!

Scotland is iconic! *Nessie* and whisky, *bagpipes*, castles and myths lure you to this wildly romantic northern country with its magnificent, scenic landscapes. On a drive through the countryside you will be rewarded with panoramic views of hills, bog lakes and steep coastlines. The Atlantic weather ensures constant changes in the sky's hue and the dramatic *Highlands* are at their most spectacular on foot. Scotland's exceptional natural environment and changeable weather left an indelible mark on its people. Their disposition has been influenced as much by historic hardship, a subarctic location and strict Calvinistic values, as by the fierce and melancholic character of their ancestors: the Celts, Scots and Picts.

It is this blend that has resulted in the Scots being more frank and impetuous than their more reserved southern neighbours, the Anglo-Saxon English. For 300 years, the two nations grew *politically closer*. Recently, two Scotsmen – Tony Blair and Gordon Brown – were even prime ministers. Today, the Scots owe their legal autonomy and independent parliament to Blair's *devolution*. In Edinburgh, currently the Scottish National Party (SNP) is in power. However, in 2014 their independence referendum failed. During the 2016 Brexit referendum the Scots voted by a majority to

Photo: Highland cattle

remain in the EU. Therefore, another referendum or other political concessions may soon emerge. The five million Scots can be confident about their future. Ship building on the River Clyde may have been key to getting Scotland's economy up to speed 150 years ago, but today its primary growth is in computer and genetic engineering in the **Silicon Glen** between Edinburgh and Glasgow. University places in Scotland are highly sought after and the country has been able to rely on innovation and an excellent education system for a long time now.

Its natural landscape is what draws most visitors to Scotland but it is also a cultural destination. In the rolling hills of the southern Lowlands, lovely towns like Jedburgh and Dryburgh nestle with the **romantic abbey ruins** as a dramatic backdrop. Gothic arches bear testimony to Scotland's border history. A bicycle tour or day hike (e.g. in Melrose) is the best way to see the country's monastery ruins and trout rivers. Abbotsford House is a must and will also put you on the trail of Scotland's literature. In the 19th century it was the fairy-tale residence of novelist **Sir Walter Scott**, to whom Scotland and the

> **Real men wear plaid skirts**

Highlands owe their fame abroad. Without Sir Walter's stories, the cliché of men in tartan kilts would never have captured the public's imagination. There would be no **Hollywood Highlander** without the Lowlander Scott; the curtain would never have been raised on Donizetti's opera 'Lucia di Lammermoor'. That said, there are many Scottish legends that are not due to Sir Walter: the legend of the Loch Ness monster; the strains of the bagpipes; the taste of distilled whisky and the charm of Sean Connery in all his 007 glory.

The imaginary line between the cities of Glasgow and Edinburgh almost forms an **urban border** between the Lowlands and Highlands. These two cities, separated by only an hour's rail journey, could not be more different. **Edinburgh** exudes a **picturesque charm**: The Royal Mile, one of Europe's most atmospheric promenades, the rankings often reach Mediterranean highs. Locals sit in its outdoor cafés in their shirtsleeves after work while curious tourists explore its alleyways. The narrow lanes and alleys are quite spooky at dusk making it easy to imagine the past witch hunts and the escapades of Dr. Jekyll and Mr. Hyde. **Glasgow** is quite different. Here the city's façade does not look as though it has been hewn from a single mould; instead neo-

6000 BC	500 BC	843	1296	1297
Mesolithic hunters and gatherers come across a land bridge to the island	Celtic tribes move into the area known as Scotland today	Kenneth MacAlpine crowned first King of the Scots	Scotland becomes an English province	William Wallace (Braveheart) expelled the English in the Battle of Stirling – he was later betrayed by Scottish nobility and executed in 1305

The iron railway bridge across the Firth of Forth near Edinburgh

classical temples vie for attention among neo-Gothic towers and art nouveau influences. If you go for a drive, the street layout is more like that of Chicago than something out of the Middle Ages. In Glasgow you will experience the Scottish way of life and temperament at its authentic best. Though the *dialect* may even have English speakers flummoxed, the street life, the music clubs, the exciting art scene and the hospitality are bound to enthral.

The *Highlands* begin north of the cities: a velvet green region, among whose high mountains (bens) the lakes (lochs), which are full of fish, shine like mirrors. The lochs are the territory of trout fishermen, while the rivers attract Scotsmen for the salmon. When travelling by car, it is difficult to avert your gaze from the wonderful panoramas and focus on the road again. To your left you may have rolling mist creeping across the peat bog while to the right you may see the reddish hide of a Highland bull gleaming against the pink heather. Sun rays may catch an isolated group of pine trees in the middle of a lake, before briefly touching the slope of a jagged peak

1314
Robert the Bruce defeated the English at Bannockburn and declared Scotland independent

1542–87
The era of Mary Queen of Scots. After an unsuccessful attempt to regain the throne she was beheaded by Queen Elizabeth I.

1692
The Glen Coe Massacre led to the death of 78 MacDonald clan members. To this dfay, on 13 February people there commemorate the dead

1707
Act of Union: the Scottish Parliament decides on a union with England, after the country is declared bankrupt

Moorlands that glow like a heathland fire

where eagles and ravens circle. The sea is never more than an hour's drive away. On the **rough and rugged west coast**, between Oban and Mallaig, the sky turns from turquoise to pink in the evening. In the east, across the small harbour of the Fife peninsula, the typical morning sea fog, the **haar**, clears up to reveal a Mediterranean-like sky. Even as a beginner you should try a **round of golf**, especially the golf courses on the east coast dunes between St Andrews, Aberdeen and Peterhead are scenic highlights, which are called **links**.

The area north of the Great Glen geological fault line and 'the Highlands capital' Fort William may **come across as deserted**. Yet the undulating purple heathlands – from August glowing like a heathland fire — are by no means a wilderness, even if here Scotland tends to appear as incredibly untamed. The **grasslands** were once covered in rustling forests and woodland. In the 19th century the woodland was cleared by

large landowners who drove off the local crofters so that they could start large-scale sheep farms and go hunting. Today you can see the **red deer** that they introduced for the hunt at the places such as the Cairngorm National Park. With no natural predators – the last Scottish wolf died well more than 260 years ago – the deer population continues to expand. A mere one per cent of the original pine forests remain today.

Travelling even further north you will reach the remote **Orkney** and **Shetland Islands** both with a distinctly different, more autonomous feel to them. Their stone circles and geographical names bear testimony to the existence of settlements almost 5000 years ago and Viking connections. The islands are very acces-

1746
The last Scottish uprising, led by the Stuart Bonnie Prince Charlie, fails at the bloody Battle of Culloden

1782–1854
During the Highland Clearances, large landowners completely displaced the population of the Scottish Highlands and introduced sheep farming. By the end of the evictions the Scottish clan system had been destroyed and Gaelic largely died out as a language in Scotland

1970
Orkney and Shetland became North Sea oil powers

sible by car if you don't mind the ferry crossing. If you **travel** west you get the Celtic Hebrides. A boat trip between the mountainous Inner Hebrides Mull, **Skye** and Rùm offers a rugged tour through the tidal swells. If you set course for the Outer Hebrides you will come across the other-worldly islands of North Uist, South Uist, and Harris — with its distinctive mountains and deserted beaches — and Lewis which has Britain's second-largest **stone circle**. These outlying islands are rather special and ideal for experiencing solitude. Visitors come here for the unique ambiance

The aurora borealis light show

created by the Northern Lights, the psychedelic **play of light** of the skies on a harshly beautiful landscape. Scotland leaves the most lasting impression when you take the time to wander off for **walks into its pristine nature**, be it along the coast or to the many ruins and castles. Always keep your hiking **boots** close at hand in your car when you travel through Britain's north.

Sandwood Bay south of Cape Wrath: one of the country's many isolated beaches

1999 Devolution brings an independent parliament and partial autonomous rule

2002 Loch Lomond and Trossachs National Park became Scotland's first national park

2011 The left-wing liberal Scottish National Party (SNP) wins a majority in parliament

2014 Despite the failure of the independence vote, the Scots win more autonomy

2016 The SNP with leader Nicola Sturgeon wins 63 of 129 seats in parliament

WHAT'S HOT

1 My home is my castle

Breathtaking solitude Scots are now attracted to immerse themselves in the solitude of their homeland – the latest trend is self-catering holidays where they can experience relative peace and quiet. But this must be stylish with a separate kitchen and panoramic outlook: such as the grass roof and wonderful amenities at *Beach Bay Cottage (tel. 0845 2 68 08 01 | www.beachbaycottage.co.uk | from £1190/week)* situated on the remote western beach on the Isle of Lewis. At Loch Duich, near Eilean Donan Castle, you can stay in the Nordic styled barn conversion *Leachachan Barn (www.leachachanbarn.net | from £650/week)* with sea views. Even more fabulous retreats in beautifully remote spots can be found at *www.wildernesscottages.co.uk*.

2 Curling

Sweep away like world champions In fact, curling, the winter sport invented in Scotland, simply means "spinning" – it's all about getting heavy granite weights spinning on the ice to hit the target. Two curling world championships will be held up to 2020 in Scotland. If you want to try it out and not just watch: the season runs from September to April at *Kinross Curling Rink (www.kinrosscurling.co.uk)* in *The Green Hotel (Kinross | Loch Leven)*. Alternatively, you can join a group and take part in beginners' classes at www.trycurling.com.

3 Tradition with a twist

Dance the Céilidh Thanks to modern influences the traditional *céilidh* (pronounced kay-lee) is being spiced up with bass and beats and is making inroads into nightclubs with traditional instruments. On a Saturday you can enjoy this social dance at *The Skipinnish Ceilidh House (34–38 George Street | Oban | www.skipinnishceilidhhouse.com)* where traditional instruments are still used but disco lights spur on the dancers. *Hud yer Wheesht* lends Gaelic music a funky element *(www.hudyerwheesht.co.uk)(photo)*. The scene's big event is the annual Battle of the Bands on the Isle of Bute *(short.travel/scot15)*.

4

The VW camper

Back to the future In Scotland VW camper vans are undergoing a revival: Old VW buses have been restored and now populate Scottish campsites. The Scots love the T2 series and have fans clubs that swap restoration tips on how to keep them going for as long as possible. Hire one from *Escape Campers (Eyvoll Cottage | Stepends Road | Lochwinnoch | www.escapecampers.co.uk)* or from *Scotland by Camper (9 Rhannan Road | Cathcart | Glasgow | bycamper.com)(photo)*.

Fitness with wellies!

5

Fitness in the great outdoors Before they weed and cultivate the landscape, the green gymers balance on one leg like storks as part of their warm-up programme. Nature-loving Brits love gardening outdoors – this is how (stressed) Scotsmen and women enhance their wellness in some beautiful outdoor locations. There are Green Gyms in towns wherever you go i.e. Aberdeen *(Foucausie | Grandhome | www.tcv.org.uk/greengym)(photo)* and west of Glasgow *(Ferguslie Sports Centre | 100 Blackstoun Road | Paisley)*, or picturesque locations near Inverness *(30 Millbank Road | Munlochy)*.

IN A NUTSHELL

CLANS

The term clan (*clann* in Gaelic) means a closely-knit group of inter-related families. Mac is the word for son in Scottish Gaelic. These old family tie terms are anything but dated and obsolete, on the contrary every year thousands of Americans or people residing in the South Pacific come to Scotland to peruse the country's archives for their family history, bearing testimony to the fact that the clan remains alive and well! Those in search of their ancestry have to go far back into the annals of history to find anything – a parliamentary decision in 1745 banned the clan system in Scotland. With this the curtain fell on a medieval social fabric that divided the Scottish identity into roughly four points of the compass. The main tribes were: the Picts from the north, the Normans from England, the Scots from Ireland and the Britains from Wales. The head of the clan had full jurisdiction over the land and lives of his clan members – leading to fierce fighting within the clans. Countless ballads also bear testimony to the fact that the clans did not like one another by any stretch of the imagination, for instance the Glen Coe massacre. Nevertheless the clans survived, at least by name. There are around five million MacDonalds (also: Macdonald, McDonald) worldwide arguably making it the most globally famous clan.

BAGPIPES

The stirring and strident skirl of the bagpipe has also been used as a

Photo: Bagpipers at the Cowal Highland Games in Dunoon

Folklore and modernity: the Scots make the balancing act between old and new seem effortless

weapon of war: inspiring the troops and unsettling the enemy. The Romans marched to it, the English had it before the Scots (possibly introduced by the Romans) and today even the Jordanian army has adopted them.The history of the bagpipe saw its turning point in the gruesome Battle of Culloden where 100 Scottish pipers were drawn and quartered.

Despite the fact that England then outlawed the bagpipe the Scottish persevered and retained their stronghold over it in much the same ingenious way they have succeeded in marketing Scotland's myths and legend.

A DIEU EU?

The Scots must now feel like they're on a different planet. Firstly, in 2014 a slim majority voted against independence from Great Britain. In 2016, they didn't want to split from Europe – 62 per cent voted against Brexit, however, they are tied to the result in Britain. Scotland's relationship with the rest of the

British Isles is complex. Should there be another referendum against rule from London? Opinion polls show that the Scots are so concerned about the economy that a new vote would fail again.

researchers: Charles Mackintosh (1766–1843) developed waterproof clothing and to this day the raincoat retains his name; John Dunlop (1840–1921) invented air-filled tyres; the steam machine

When the local derby – Celtic versus Rangers – is held in Glasgow, the fans go to pray at the stadium

Scotland's determined leader, Nicola Sturgeon, therefore doesn't exactly want to ask, even if she wants to avoid Theresa May's so-called hard Brexit.

The reason is that Scotland needs EU funding and EU migrants to maintain its economy that it now controls independently. Nicola versus Theresa: an exciting match. Nobody will lose their heads, however, like in the days of Queen Elizabeth I and Mary Stuart.

INNOVATORS

Bacteriologist Alexander Fleming (born in 1881) discovered penicillin after extensive research which earned him the Nobel Prize for Medicine. Scotland has produced not only physicians and

goes back to James Watt (1736–1819) and Alexander Graham Bell (1847–1922) was the father of the telephone. There is an explanation for why such a small country has been so blessed with such genius. In 1546 the reformer John Knox insisted on compulsory schooling. Scotland's high academic standard has been maintained to this day – be it innovations in the field of micro-electronics in the Silicon Glen or in scientific tests to manipulate genetic material (here Dolly the cloned sheep springs to mind).

JAMES MEETS HARRY

For many people their discovery of Scotland began in the cinema with the Highlands being used again and again as the backdrop to large film productions. 'Highlander' with Christopher Lambert is partly set in Eilean Donan Castle. Glen Nevis and Glen Coe were the film locations where Mel Gibson, as 'Braveheart', beat the English. In 'Skyfall', James Bond later called in. Harry Potter steamed over the viaduct in the Hogwarts Express steam train and on the Glenfinnan line from Fort William to Mallaig.

Doune Castle near Stirling appears in 'Game of Thrones' – this and Edinburgh are also the film settings for the TV series 'Outlander'. In 2017, Danny Boyle created the sequel to 'Trainspotting' (1996) – 'T2 Trainspotting' was also mainly filmed in Edinburgh.

KICK IT LIKE CELTIC

In Glasgow football is almost a substitute religion. The championship trophy goes back and forth between Celtic – the team founded by Irish Catholic immigrants – and Rangers who are largely Protestant. If you happen to wander through Glasgow East, a poorer part of the city, you ought to drop in at one of the pubs signposted with a green Celtic banner. In all probability the video showing Celtic Glasgow's defeat of Inter Milan in the European Cup of 1967 will be on the screen as you step inside. See *www.rangers.co.uk* or *www.celticfc.co.uk*. In 2012, Rangers were relegated due to massive debts. Since 2016, their fortunes have revived.

GOING GREEN

The Scottish National Party's grasp of power with Alex Salmond as First Minister (Prime Minister) seems to have heralded in an ecological era in Scotland. There have been signs of increasing environmental consciousness and a heavy drive to the expansion of re-newable energies. Europe's largest wind farm is 15 km/9.3 mi from Glasgow and supplies electricity to 180,000 households and there are also investments being made in offshore energy and wave power. Up to 2032, the electricity supply is to be generated exclusively from sustainable sources and the last nuclear power station is to be closed. It is Scotland's ambitious goal that renewable energies make up 80 per cent of the country's electricity needs by 2020. As a visitor to the country this wave of environmental consciousness is however not that apparent as yet. Many hotels and guest houses still have old sash windows instead of double glazing and the cholesterol-rich Scottish breakfast is a far cry from organic and healthy nutrition. Even so, the environmentally conscious age is increasingly making inroads into tourism and the oval green sign with the wording Green Tourism is often seen in the entrances to accommodation, tourist attractions, restaurants and public buildings. Businesses throughout the United Kingdom are awarded the green label for sustainable and ecological management. See www.green-business.co.uk

HIGHLAND DRAMAS

For visitors, the Highlands begin north of the Glasgow–Edinburgh line, and for the Scots, who are geographically correct, the border runs to the Lowlands from the Clyde estuary near Glasgow in an arc to the Moray Firth north-west of Inverness. The English multimillionaire Paul Lister caused a stir in the Highlands back in 2003 when he bought the Alladale Estate near Ardgay north of Inverness. His plan was to revive the original habitat on the 25,000-acre estate. Although the mountain landscape is dramatic, it is also a

Kilted and muscle-bound – a typical Games participant

desert in ecological terms. At the latest since large sheep farmers drove out local crofters during the infamous Highland Clearances, also introduced deer for hunting and finally ruining the native scots pine forests by deforestation, the Highlands revealed their bare, uninviting face. Paul Lister, with the help of experts, reintroduced elks, planted hundreds of thousands of trees, culled the rapidly growing deer population and built lodges that blend gently into the landscape (see p. 67).

STRONG MEN IN KILTS

Centuries ago when the king was in search of new bodyguards, or when clan chiefs met, they held a kind of Olympic Games for strong men: the Highland Games. These are still held today, with 100 throughout Scotland showcasing more than 40 disciplines. *Tossing the caber* is when kilted muscle men throw a tree trunk and get it to somersault a few times. *Throwing the hammer* is a heavy metal ball attached to a cane handle while *putting the stone* is similar to shot put. There are also more lightfooted disciplines, such as a Highlands tap dance. The Games of course are also where the best bagpipe players can be heard. The most famous take place in Braemar at the beginning of September under the auspices of the Queen.

CELTISH HERITAGE

'Slàinte' say the Scots when they mean 'cheers'! The word is Gaelic – an old Celtic idiom that has survived in some corners of Scotland. The Outer Hebrides and northern west coast still have pockets where Gaelic is spoken and understood. On the Western Isles, even the road signs are bilingual – there are Gaelic language radio and TV programmes and school lessons. About one per cent of Scots speak fluent Gaelic. Important words for visitors are *glen* (narrow valley), *ben* (mountain), *loch* (lake), *kyle* (straits), *close* (alleyway).

MORE THAN MAGICAL

Scottish literature is dominated by an impressive triumvirate: Sir Walter Scott, Robert Louis Stevenson and Robert Burns. Burns (1759–96), poet of the pubs and drinking holes, is Scotland's national poet. In his honour, on 25 January many Scots eat haggis with sheep's stomach; wash it down with whisky and recite their Burns. Sir Walter Scott's (1771–1832) legacy continues in his romantic novels while Robert Louis Stevenson's (1850–94) 'Treasure Island' among other novels has secured him a place in bookshelves worldwide. Since 1987, Ian Rankin's cult Detective Rebus is active on Edinburgh's crime scene. The elective Scotswoman and former unemployed Joanne K. Rowling became a multimillionaire with her seven Harry Potter novels that were published until 2007.

THE SOUND OF SCOTLAND

Contemporary Scotland is also known for its melodious rock and the popular band Franz Ferdinand from Glasgow (which has absolutely nothing to do with the Habsburg Archduke) is a great example of the phenomenon. This indie Scottish rock band seem to have a very similar beginnings to that of some other Scottish bands i.e. a combination of study at the Glasgow School of Art and believe it or not, a drunken brawl. Other bands and musicians from the heart of the country such as Belle & Sebastian, Travis, Delgado, Simple Minds and Amy Macdonald are similarly successful – their unique indie sounds are melancholic at times but always distinctly Scottish in tone.

TARTANS AND KILTS

Tartan and kilt refer to the check patterned skirt that is typically worn by the Scots. Tartan is the pattern that indicates membership of a clan. To make the skirt-like kilt a length of tartan (6–8 yds) is pleated and wrapped around the waist, the family clan determines the tartan, the chilly weather calls for knee high socks, while a small knife in the sock ensures that small repairs can be conducted. Kilts were once the perfect outfit for the poor inhabitants of the marshy Highlands but after the Battle of Culloden in 1746 kilts were banned. Offenders of the new Dress Act decree faced imprisonment and even banishment. In 1782 the ban was lifted and the kilt allowed but the old patterns had long been forgotten. Today the kilt is worn primarily at ceremonies and weddings. Ask a Scotsman what he is wearing under his kilt and he may do a cartwheel to satisfy your curiosity!

SCOTTISH POUND

The British pound is legal tender in Scotland; however you cannot pay for your purchases with the Scottish pound in the rest of the United Kingdom. The Scottish pound is printed by several institutions and therefore the images on the notes can differ for the 5, 10, 20, 50 and 100 pound notes. The Royal Bank of Scotland additionally brings out notes to the value of 1 pound. Featured on Scottish currency are the poet Robert Burns, the Firth of Forth Bridge, whisky and Orkney's Stone Age treasures.

FOOD & DRINK

The Scottish start their day with a hearty cooked breakfast that can include *kippers*, smoked herring or haddock. Also on the breakfast menu are oat *porridge* and *oatcakes* – a savoury oat biscuit cooked on the griddle or baked – and Orkney is renowned for the best!

Today hotel guests can eschew the Scottish breakfast and choose the *continental breakfast* instead. Many B&Bs nowadays also serve this lighter breakfast option.

In comparison to breakfast, Scottish lunch tends to be a light snack such as a sandwich or homemade soup (broth) at the pub or your proverbial *fish and chips* wrapped in a newspaper.

Scottish *high tea* is a traditional culinary delight served between 4pm and 5pm in the afternoon and plays itself out as an opulent unhurried feast not to be missed. This is not a delicate cup of green tea and a biscuit, but rather the finest in Ceylon teas accompanied by an array of mouth-watering sandwiches and pastries and freshly baked *scones* served with jam and cream.

If you meet up for dinner later on (from about 7pm) expect only the finest of the island's produce as Scotland's cuisine is experiencing a new lease on life. For years Scottish cuisine had to contend with a poor reputation. If the truth be told, lots of locals still indulge in the mighty *Scottish breakfast* without giving their health a second thought. However, a growth in Scotland's economy, and flourishing tourism in the cities, has ensured the expansion of the country's

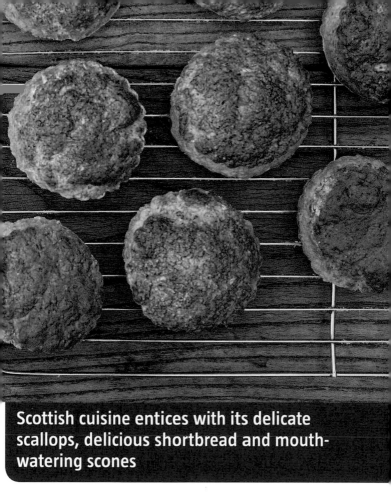

Scottish cuisine entices with its delicate scallops, delicious shortbread and mouth-watering scones

culinary repertoire. In Glasgow and Edinburgh you'll find the whole spectrum of restaurants from sushi to Mexican (and of course vegetarian) and the wealthy middle class have also embraced healthy *Mediterranean cuisine*. Chic Italian restaurants are guaranteed to be bursting at the seams at night and in the cities there are countless delis selling Scottish salmon alongside Parma ham and balsamic vinegar.

So what is typical Scottish cuisine? However you define it, one thing is certain: it has changed for the better. The reason for this is the return to high-grade locally grown produce. Top chef Claire MacDonald has been instrumental in generating *greater creativity* in the kitchen not only on her television programme but with her popular cookbooks. Long before other chefs endorsed local produce she promoted the use of wild mushrooms from the forests in Kingussie and beef from the Highlands and championed local cattle breeds such as Aberdeen-Angus, Galloway, Longhorn, Shorthorn and Highland.

LOCAL SPECIALITIES

Arbroath smokies – smoked haddock served warm, named after a fishing village on the east coast

atholl brose – the ingredients of this punch include oatmeal brose, honey, whisky and cream, traditionally served on New Year's Eve

black pudding – the famous blood and oat sausage comes from Stornoway in the Outer Hebrides

cairnsmore – a nutty hard cheese made from sheep's milk, the perfect end to a meal

cock-a-leekie – a hearty chicken and leek soup popular at the coast and on the islands

cranachan – a delectable dessert of fresh raspberries, honey and whipped cream served in a glass with a dash of whisky for good measure

cullen skink – a hearty, creamy soup of smoked haddock, onion, milk and potato

deep-fried Mars bar – ice cold Mars bar dipped in batter and fried, not an urban myth!

haggis – Scotland's national dish has gained international fame thanks to Robert Burns. Offal minced with onion, bread, spices, eggs and flour encased in a sheep's stomach and left to simmer. Although opinions may vary it is worth a try in a good restaurant (photo right)

hotchpotch – a hearty lamb and mixed vegetable stew, popular in the Borders region

roastit Bubbly-Jock – Christmas turkey stuffed with oysters and chestnuts

skirlie – dish made with oatmeal fried with onion and seasoning

stovies – this dish owes its name to the stove on which it is cooked. It is a lamb or beef potato stew that is perfect for a cold day and best served with a glass of ice cold buttermilk

Regional produce has been the key to the renaissance in Scotland's upscale restaurant cuisine. Scotland now has **14 Michelin stars** that attest to the high quality of its restaurants – four of these have been awarded to restaurants in Edinburgh. Martin Wishart is known as an especially pioneering cook, he holds stars in Leith and in Balloch at Loch Lomond. The sought-after ranking has even gone to some small country hotels in remote regions such as *The Peat Inn (closed Mon | tel. 01334 84 02 06 | Expensive)* in the centre of the Fife

A feast for the senses: whisky has 800 aromas

peninsula, the *Knockinaam Lodge (daily | tel. 01776 81 04 71 | www.knockinaam lodge.com | Expensive)* near Stranrear and Claire MacDonald's *Kinloch Lodge (daily | Sleat | tel. 01471 83 33 33 | Expensive)* on Skye where Brazilian Marcello Tully is the head chef.

The harmonious combination of nature, romantic fireplaces and Michelin-star cuisine makes Scotland a very attractive destination even in the winter when it is worth looking out for special package deals. Gourmet cuisine has also left its mark on some of the more rural pubs and, by all accounts, on eating out in the cities. Daily specials with two or three course menus are great value for money. Fresh *fish* is a sought-after speciality of Scottish cuisine. On a trip along the east coast you will come across small towns like Arbroath where the smell of burning charcoal and sea salt lingers in the air. Fishing boats are anchored in the harbour and *lobster traps* can be seen all along the pier. The smokehouses produce smoked halibut and salmon – freshly caught and cured – that is absolutely delicious! However, most chefs prefer fish from the cleaner west coast where the lobsters and shellfish are of a higher quality.

Despite its vast culinary repertoire there is one thing that is missing in Scotland: its own vineyards. Cellar masters have to order in from Italy, Spain, South Africa, California and of course France – it's a fact that Leith (Edinburgh's port) is the destination for some of the finest Bordeaux.

As wine is best served with *cheese* it should naturally be one of Scotland's own. Try the *Lanark Blue*, which looks like Gorgonzola. It is made from sheep's milk from the Borders region and is creamy white with blue veining. Also highly recommended is the *White Diamond* from the Galloway region, a delicate and mild cream cheese that goes perfectly with strawberries.

SHOPPING

Are you looking for something more unique than a kilt made from acrylic, a woollen jumper that shrinks after the first wash, or a whisky that you can often find cheaper at home? It's best to browse in the wonderful specialist shops of genuine craftsmen, weavers and in the local distilleries.

CASHMERE

Scotland is well known for its top quality light-weight cashmere knitwear such as cardigans and vests and prices are good as the wool is imported on a large scale. You need look no further than *Johnstons of Elgin (Mon–Thu 10am–4pm | Visitor Centre | New Mill | Elgin | www.johnston scashmere.com)* which is said to have the best quality and you can buy directly on location.

DESIGN

You will find poetic and surreal textiles, lampshades and wallpaper at designers *Timorous Beasties (384 Great Western Road | www.timorousbeasties.com)* – the shop's name is taken from a Robert Burns poem – the creative team studied at the Glasgow School of Art and opened their store in the same town. In Edinburgh you will come across a varied and witty selection of young Scottish designers at the *Concrete Wardrobes* cooperative *(50a Broughton Street | www.concretewardrobe.com)*.

KILTS

The kilt is actually a very comfortable piece of clothing and it is fast catching on among Scotland's younger generation with many following tradition and wearing it for weddings and festivals. The kilt is also experiencing a revival in the cities, albeit with some less traditional versions, such as those made from black leather, silk or even PVC. You will find amazing kilts – both traditional or completely over the top – at *Howard Nickelby's* shop with the telling name *21st Century Kilts (48 Thistle St | Edinburgh | tel. 07774 75 72 22 | www.21stcenturykilts.com)*.

TWEED

Only sheep's wool spun on the Outer Hebrides and handwoven in cottage industries on the islands can carry the Harris Tweed *(www.harristweed.org)* label.

The Kilt is iconic – and whisky is a taste of Scotland for connoisseurs. Tradition is firmly on the shopping list

The local Harris Tweed Authority certifies and monitors its production. The resilient cloth with its herringbone pattern has been produced on the islands of Harris and Lewis for centuries. Noble tailors in Edinburgh and London then turn it into coats and waistcoats and other garments. Rough and old-fashioned? That's not true! The weaver Donald John Mackay, from the coastal village of Luskentyre on Harris, made headlines when Nike purchased miles of material from him for the manufacture of a retro sports shoe. Tweed is catwalk material and its sophisticated look is ideal for accessories like handbags. Nowadays, this classic woollen weave no longer has muted colours: the weavers in the tiny houses on Harris love giving traditional tweed vibrant colours. *www.luskentyreharristweed.co.uk*

WHISKY

Scotland has made malt whisky an incredible export bestseller. Unblended single malts (see p. 74) admittedly account for just 10 per cent of whisky production, yet they are internationally famous.

That makes people curious to know the carefully guarded secret of the 110 distilleries. If you buy whisky at the distillery, it's generally not cheaper than in a supermarket, but you can enjoy a guided tour and even get a sweatshirt. You can also taste a wide range of products, even the youngest blends with fantastic names and special bottles designed to entice new clientele. The shop area is usually where floor malting is done: *Laphroaig, Bowmore* and *Kilchoman* on the *Isle of Islay*, *Highland Park* on Orkney, *Springbank* in Campbelltown and *The Balvenie* and *Benriach* in Speyside.

Edradour near Pitlochry is tiny and quaint, while the distilleries on Islay and Skye make the most of their coastal location.

THE SOUTH

The excitement slowly builds as you approach Scotland by car ferry from Amsterdam to Newcastle upon Tyne in north-east England. **This has been a border area ever since the Romans built Hadrian's Wall, a demarcation line to the north.**

The wall was to prevent incursions by the Picts and the Scots to present day Scotland. Fortress ruins like *Caerlaverock Castle* at Dumfries are evidence of the battles between the English and the Scots some 1000 years later, as are strongholds like *Smailholm Tower* in the hilly Lowlands or Southern Uplands – another name for the area from Edinburgh to Glasgow. Compared to the deserted Highlands, the Lowlands are characterised by beautiful small towns such as Melrose, Jedburgh and Kelso where romantic abbey ruins are a reminder of Scotland's Catholic past. The area's country roads are popular with cyclists and the coastal footpath, the *Southern Uplands Way*, attracts ramblers and hikers. The Lowlands are divided into the western region of Dumfries and Galloway and the Borders region to the east. In the west you can walk in the footsteps of the national poet, Robert Burns. In Galloway the coastal section, tempered by the mild Gulf Stream climate, is well worth a visit, especially the *Galloway Forest Park*. The Borders is also where you will find Sir Walter Scott's home, *Abbotsford* where he created the novels that brought him worldwide acclaim.

Romantic Lowlands: stay on the trail of Scotland's famous poets and explore castles and ancient abbeys

BORDERS REGION

In south-eastern Scotland, a lush green landscape of rolling hills stretches out between Edinburgh, Moffat and the English border, offering both great scenic beauty and a turbulent history. Fly fishermen stand up to their chest in water on the rivers Tweed, Esk, Teviot and Ettrick. The romantic sight of Early Gothic abbey ruins, dream castles and fortified towers in and around small towns like Melrose, Jedburgh, Kelso, Selkirk and Peebles are a delightful contrast to natural wonders you can hike to, such as the Grey Mare's Tail waterfall and the exhilarating coastal cliffs of St Abb's Head. It was the charming Borders region scenery, and the history of bitter border wars fought with England in the late Middle Ages, that formed the backdrop of Sir Walter Scott's historical novels. Hollywood films featuring Scotland, operas and the tourist industry in Scotland are all thanks to Scott's influence.

19th century author Theodor Fontane expressed his contempt for Sir Walter's

Sir Walter Scott's desk in Abbotsford House: just as he left it

SIGHTSEEING

ABBOTSFORD HOUSE ★
(127 E3) (*Ⓜ L14*)

In 1812 novelist Sir Walter Scott (1771–1832) acquired the estate on the River Tweed and built his Victorian-style dream castle. Visitors can view the desk at which he wrote the more than 40 novels that captivated the imagination of readers worldwide. Integral to his subject matter is Scottish folklore seen in many of his works such as 'Lucia of Lammermuir' (which was turned into an opera by Donizetti), 'The Heart of Midlothian' and 'Waverley'. His urge to write may also stem from a mountain of debt. Collectors' items still showcased in Abbotsford House today include the sword of freedom fighter Rob Roy, the chalice Bonnie Prince Charlie drank from and countless other memorabilia from Scotland's rich history. On his visit, the German late

hoarding. But it is precisely the authenticity of the novelist's Scottish abode that has made it a draw card with tourists from around the world who come to see Scott's world, where he may literally have written himself to ill health. His favourite spot is in the nearby Eildon Hills and is now known as ⋇ *Scott's View. March, Nov daily 10am–4pm, April–Oct daily 10am–5pm, Dec–Feb closed | £9.60 | www.scottsabbotsford.com | 4 km/2.5 mi south-east of Galashiels*

A708 ★ (126 C4) (*Ⓜ K–L14*)

A dream road: if you take the A708 from Moffat towards Galashiels and to the Border abbeys, you may think that you are already in the Highlands. The scenery surrounding the impressive *Grey Mare's Tail* waterfall is by far the most mountainous and the hike up to the waterfall source in INSIDER TIP Loch Skeen is well worth it. After the steep climb you can enjoy a swim. The view on the ❄️ way down is spectacular. Carry on driving 8 km/5 mi to *Tibbie Shiel's Inn (St Mary's Loch | Budget)*, the perfect stop for a cup of coffee. Even the authors Sir Walter Scott and James Hogg (1770–1835) came here to relax and chat and Hogg's statue overlooks the delightful *St Mary's Loch*.

BORDERS RAILWAY (127 D1–3) *(📖 L13)*
On the re-opened line the train rattles back and forth every day, several times an hour between Edinburgh, Galashiels and Tweedbank near Melrose. Sometimes, the steam train even runs with a buffet car *(April–Oct Wed, Thu, Sun | from £40). Tickets from £11.20 | www.scotrail.co.uk/scotland-by-rail/borders-railway*

DRYBURGH ABBEY (127 E3) *(📖 M14)*
Sir Walter Scott's resting place beneath mighty cedars since 1832. The most romantic among the Borders abbeys is an early Gothic Premonstratensian abbey dating back to 1150 located alongside the River Tweed. *April–Sept daily 9.30am–5.30pm, Oct–March daily 10am–4pm | £5.50 | 8 km/5 mi south-east of Melrose*

HERMITAGE CASTLE (127 D4) *(📖 L15)*
It's haunted! The lonely landscape of the surrounding area makes the mighty ramparts of this partly derelict fortress from the 13th century look even more imposing. Even those immune to feeling frightened shudder at the thought of violent battles and Shakespearean-style dramas.
Mary Queen of Scots rode all the way here in 1566 to take care of her beloved Bothwell, a feat that almost killed her. *April–Sept daily 9.30am–5.30pm | £4.50 | www.historicenvironment.scot | 10 km/6.2 mi south of Hawick*

JEDBURGH ABBEY ★
(127 E3–4) *(📖 M14)*
The best preserved and most impressive abbey ruin of the four great Borders' abbeys. Augustinian monks have led a monastic life here since the 12th century.

With audio-visual account and excavation pieces. *Opening times and website same as Dryburgh Abbey / Jedburgh / £5.50 / www.historicenvironment.scot*

MELROSE ABBEY (127 D–E3) *(ꟼ L14)*
The ruins of the abbey, that King David I had built for the French Cistercians in 1136, are in Melrose, the most beautiful Borders village. The abbey was built with a special resting place for what was believed to be the heart of Scotland's national hero, Robert the Bruce. A 9 km/5.6 mi trail from the town takes hikers to the surrounding 🔆 *Eildon Hills* with their breathtaking views of the River Tweed and the abbey. *April–Sept daily 9.30am–5.30pm, Oct–March daily 10am–4pm | £5.50 | www.historicenvironment.scot*

SMAILHOLM TOWER (127 E3) *(ꟼ M14)*
This is an excellent example of a 15th century fortified Borders residential tower.

Visible for miles, it stands on a dramatic crag as a reminder of the Border Wars. Today it houses a tapestries and costumes exhibition. *April–Sept daily 9.30am–5.30pm | £4.50 | www.historicenvironment.scot | 9 km/5.6 mi west of Kelso*

ST ABB'S HEAD ★ (127 F2) *(ꟼ N13)*
A dizzy drama set on the east coast which is inhabited by thousands of seabirds nesting on the grassy slopes and cliffs. It is one of Scotland's most beautiful coastal wildlife reserves (butterflies galore!) and is especially captivating in the early morning mist or at twilight. Stay over in Eyemouth or in Coldingham. *www.nnr-scotland.org.uk/st-abbs-head | 10 km/6.2 mi north of Eyemouth*

TRAQUAIR HOUSE ★ (127 D3) *(ꟼ L13)*
Originally a hunting lodge, this cosy country house and beautiful park dates

Last royal resting place beneath Gothic arches: Melrose Abbey

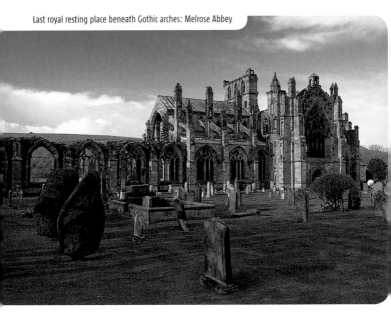

back to 1107. It has been home to the Jacobite Catholic Maxwell-Stuart family for centuries and Mary, Queen of Scots, also spent the night. Some of the memorabilia accumulated by the family over the years is on display – in some parts fascinating and in others rather kitsch. End your excursion with a glass of house ale in the inviting beer garden or spend a night at the adjoined B&B. *March–Sept daily 11am–5pm, Oct daily 11am–4pm, Nov Sat/Sun 11am–3pm | £8.80 | Innerleithen | www.traquair.co.uk*

the meditative art of *fly fishing* – whatever the weather – have come to the right place. *From £69 half-day | Transport possible from Edinburgh | www.tweedguide.com*

CYCLING
The roads in the borders region offer wonderfully undulating terrain with marked routes from 8–400 km/5–249 mi. *Cycle hire from £22 per day | For more info about routes and rentals visit www.cyclescottishborders.com*

FOOD & DRINK

BORN IN THE BORDERS
(127 E4) (*M14*)
The old farm is the new culinary centre for the borders region. Don't miss a visit to the microbrewery: Wild Harvest is an interesting beer that contains locally foraged ingredients. Essential shopping at the delicatessen shop. Plus, stylish glamping spots across the river. *Daily 10am–5pm. | Lanton | near Jedburgh | tel. 01835 83 04 95 | www.borninthebordders.com*

MARMION'S (127 D–E3) (*L14*)
A relaxed bistro opposite Melrose Abbey that serves tasty light meals, especially recommended for vegetarians. *Closed Sun | 5 Buccleuch Street | Melrose | tel. 01896 82 22 45 | www.marmionsbrasserie.co.uk | Moderate*

SPORTS & ACTIVITIES

FLY FISHING ●
Grayling, trout and salmon (Oct/Nov) splash around in the wild in the River Tweed that runs through the borders region. Visitors keen to enjoy a few hours or entire day learning how to handle a long two-handed fly rod, and to practise

WHERE TO STAY

CASTLE VENLAW (127 C3) (*L13*)
This hotel (only from the age of 16) is a 250 year old castle with a tower and offers suites with four-poster beds and a cosy bar. Very romantic and therefore a favourite among couples on honeymoon. *Edinburgh Road, Peebles | tel. 01721 72 40 66 | www.venlaw.co.uk | Expensive*

EDENWATER HOUSE
(127 E3) (*M13*)
For the romantics among their guests hoteliers Jeff and Jacqui Kelly will gladly light a few extra candles. You get the feeling that this couple really enjoy the hospitality industry. Jacqui is a superb chef *(Moderate)* and the quiet atmosphere of the old vicarage with beautiful garden as well as the inviting rooms will make you want to extend your stay. There is a separate smoking lounge. *4 rooms | Bridge Street | Ednam near Kelso | tel. 01573 22 40 70 | www.edenwaterhouse.co.uk | Moderate*

INFORMATION
There are Tourist Information Centres in all the towns mentioned: *short.travel/scot11*

DUMFRIES

(126 B–C5) (◫ K15) The largest small town in the south-west has a population of 33,000 in a tranquil location on the River Nith.

In south-eastern Dumfries & Galloway district you can follow the trail of Scotland's national poet, Robert Burns. On poetry routes, you will find wonderful ruins, art in the landscape, the wild southern coast and not forgetting black-and-white cows.

SIGHTSEEING

BURNS' HOUSE
Poet Robert Burns (1759–96) spent the last three years of his life in this sandstone house. The father of twelve worked as a tax collector. His wife Jean Armour lived here until 1834 so that the house really ought to have been named after her. On display is Burns' study and various memorabilia. *April–Sept Mon–Sat 10am–5pm, Sun 2pm–5pm, Oct–March Tue–Sat 10am–1pm and 2pm–5pm | admission free | Burns Street*

DUMFRIES MUSEUM ⚘
The highlight of this museum is the camera obscura (£3.20) built into the top floor of the old windmill. In good weather you can see panoramic views of the town. *April–Sept Mon–Sat 10am–5pm, Sun 2pm–5pm, Oct–March Tue–Sat 10am–1pm and 2pm–5pm | admission free*

FOOD & DRINK

GLOBE INN
A beer and pub lunch at Robert Burns' local haunt is a must if you're a fan. But be warned: sit in his favourite chair and

you will end up having to order a round of drinks for everyone in the pub! *56 High Street | tel. 01387 25 23 35 | Budget*

WHERE TO STAY

CORSEWALL LIGHTHOUSE
(125 D5) (◫ G16)
This old lighthouse tower has been beaming its warning across Scotland's south-west coast for two centuries. Move in! The first-rate suites and rooms are well-furnished. Guaranteed to be highlights of your stay: the dramatic sea views and the five-course menu served in such a unique location. *11 rooms | Stranraer | tel. 01776 85 32 20 | www.lighthousehotel.co.uk | Expensive*

STEAMBOAT INN
Quaint country pub with boating atmosphere. Pleasant B&B rooms, delicious fish dishes. Ten minutes by car to the romantic ruins of Sweetheart *Abbey. 2 rooms | Carsethorn | 21 km/13.1 mi south of Dumfries | tel. 01387 88 06 31 | www.steamboatinn.co.uk | Moderate*

INFORMATION

DUMFRIES & GALLOWAY TOURIST BOARD
64 Whitesands | Dumfries | Tel. 01387 25 38 62 | www.visitdumfriesandgalloway.co.uk

WHERE TO GO

CAERLAVEROCK CASTLE ★ ●
(126 C6) (◫ K15)
Out of a fairy tale: this charming triangular fortress ruin surrounded by a moat is 13 km/8.1 mi south of Dumfries. It dates back to the medieval Border wars and has imposing ramparts (the damage to the masonry was probably done

in the last siege) and a Renaissance fa-çade was added to it in the 17th century – in the evening it makes for the perfect backdrop to a **INSIDER TIP** romantic picnic. Alongside it, there is a huge bird sanctuary in the marshlands of the Solway Firth that is ideal for a walk. Why not visit in winter? *April–Sept daily 9.30am–5.30pm, Oct–March 9.30am–4.30pm | £5.50 | Glencaple | www.historicenvronment.scot*

CULZEAN CASTLE ☀ (125 D3) (*ω H14*)

Perched on a cliff this manor house is located 70 km/43.5 mi north-west of Dumfries. Landscaped gardens take you into its elegant interior with an impressive curved staircase. The castle and park are at their most spectacular in the evening bathed in the sunset. Some may find the entrance fee a little steep. *Castle: April–Oct daily 10.30am–5pm, park year-round untll sunset | house and park £15.50, park £10 | www.nts.org.uk/CulzeanCastle*

GALLOWAY FOREST PARK

(125 E4) (*ω H15*)

Nature at its best: Great Britain's largest forest park lies near Newton Stewart. Take a hike to *Bruce's Stone* on Loch Trool which commemorates Robert the Bruce's victory over the English in 1307. Plenty of informative material available at the *Glentrool Visitor Centre* – cake and snacks also on sale. *Admission free | www.gallowayforestpark.com*

INSIDER TIP GLENKILN RESERVOIR SCULPTURE PARK (126 B5) (*ω K15*)

Sir William Keswick's Sculpture Park in the middle of nowhere is open to those that can find it. In a glen you'll come across statues by sculptors such as Henry Moore, Jacob Epstein and Auguste Rodin. Sir William Keswick, a Scottish industrialist, had the park commissioned in the early 1950s. It surrounds Glenkiln Reservoir. The famous Henry Moore bronze 'King and Queen' is on a hillside above the lake. Be prepared to hike

Traders and farmers at the Dumfries Agricultural Show

some distance to enjoy the works as the park stretches over around 6 km/3.7 mi. *10 km/6.2 mi north-west of Dumfries at Shawhead*

GRETNA GREEN (127 D6) (*m̶ L15*)
This small town is world famous for its Old Blacksmith's Shop where for 200 years minors could tie the knot without parental consent. Young lovers would flee to Gretna Green across the border

is sub-tropical and even tropical. The fragrance and climate will tantalize your senses *(15 March–Oct daily 10am–5pm | £6.50)*. Another reason for a detour is the Michelin star restaurant *(5-course meal Moderate–Expensive | booking essential!)* and exceptional country hotel *Knockinaam Lodge (10 rooms | Portpatrick | tel. 01776 810471 | www.knockinaamlodge.com | Expensive)*. The bar stocks more than 150 whiskies.

Buddha statue in Samyé Ling

from England to take advantage of Scotland's less rigid marriage policies. The local blacksmith was the commissioner of oaths who performed the weddings – the blacksmith forge is now a museum (Old Blacksmith's Shop). Gretna Green remains a very popular wedding destination. However, today the bride and groom have to be at least 16 years old. *www.gretnagreen.org | approx. 25 km south-east of Dumfries*

LOGAN BOTANIC GARDENS
(125 D6) (*m̶ G16*)
Idyllic conditions on the gulf stream! In the remote south-west, the vegetation

LOW KIRKBRIDE FARM ⊘
(126 B5) (*m̶ K15*)
This is an eco-friendly cattle and sheep farm offering lovely rooms. The cattle farmed here are the Belted Galloways, an old Scottish heritage breed with a distinctive white belt around their stomachs. *6 rooms | near Glenmidge, 16 km/9.9 mi north of Dumfries | tel. 01387 820258 | www.goruralscotland.com/lowkirkbride | Budget*

ROBERT BURNS BIRTHPLACE
MUSEUM (125 E3) (*m̶ H14*)
Robert Burns was born in a cottage in Alloway on 25 January 1759. In 2011 a

large, new museum dedicated to the Scottish national hero and poet was opened. The museum is set in 10 acres of countryside, and constructed of wood that lets in a lot of natural light, just as Burns would have wanted. There are interactive displays, original manuscripts, 5000 items of memorabilia paying tribute to the author of Auld Lang Syne as well as contemporary art. *Daily 10am–5pm | £9 | Murdoch's Lone | Alloway | Ayr | www.burnsmuseum.org.uk*

(126 C–D4) (*ꟍ L14–15*)

Feel Scottish karma! In the idyllic, tranquil Esk Valley, 45 km/28 mi north-east of Dumfries, the Tibetan Centre for Buddhism and culture has been situated since 1967. The centre has about 60 residents. Visitors can stay the night (£29) and take part in morning prayers or stay longer for courses on meditation, Buddhism and gardening. *Eskdalemuir | tel. 01387 373232 | www.samyeling.org*

SCOTTISH RIVIERA
(126 B–C6) (*ꟍ K16*)

The A710 coastal road from Dumfries to Castle Douglas takes you along the scenic Scottish Riviera, past placid bays, beautiful beaches and wonderful views. The oddly shaped, snow-white lighthouse of Southerness is well worth a detour. When you reach Rockcliffe you should park your car and take the mile hike along the bay to Kippford where you end up at the *Anchor Inn (tel. 01556 620205 | Budget)* at the small harbour where you'll be served excellent pub food.

WIGTOWN BAY (125 E–F6) (*ꟍ J16*)

Now this is a remote spot, but the detour is worth it. The small town of *Wigtown* is Scotland's *National Book Town* – you can take your pick from a quarter of million

books. At the end of September it hosts a ten-day book festival *(www.wigtownbookfestival.com)*. Further south is the town of *Whithorn* and the *Whithorn Trust's Visitor Story Centre* where you'll find excavations dating back to the founder of Scottish Christendom: St Ninian was the Pict's apostle in the 5th century.

Next to the Whithorn Story Visitor Centre *(Easter–Oct daily 10.30am–5pm)* you will find the famous delicatessen *Ravenstone Deli (Tue–Sat)*, where you can feast on local venison, homemade sausage, pies and Mediterranean delicacies. The atmospheric pub *Steam Packet Inn (10 rooms | approx. 60 km/37.3 mi west of Dumfries | tel. 01988 500334 | www.steampackertinn.biz | Budget)* is a few miles further right on the bay and has simple rooms (booking advisable!).

LOW BUDGET

Kirk Yetholm Friends of Nature House *(22 beds | tel. 01573 420639 | www.syha.org.uk)* in the eastern Borders is ideal for hikers (Pennine Way) and cyclists on the Scottish Borders Cycle Route.

For a value for money breakfast look no further than *Damascus Drum Café & Bookshop* serving delicious Mediterranean cuisine, bagels, breakfasts and ⊗ fair trade coffee *(daily | 2 Silver Street | Hawick | tel. 07707 856123)*.

First-class fish and chips at *Giacopazzi's & Oblo's Bistro* on the harbour *(daily | at the Fish Market | Eyemouth | tel. 01890 752527)* and award-winning, homemade ice cream as an extra.

EDINBURGH & GLASGOW

Scotland's biggest city – Glasgow (pop. 600,000) – and its capital city, Edinburgh (pop. 500,000), line up geographically and are separated by only an hour's rail journey. Over the next decade, they will grow closer; more than 2 million people already live in the metropolitan central belt.

However, the two cities are also very different: Edinburgh exudes historic and poetic charm. Its impressive setting and chic urban architecture make it one of Europe's most attractive city destinations. Glasgow's post-industrial style is more robust and mercantile, while its skyline is more linear. Here, people became wealthy due to trade and shipbuilding on the River Clyde. The informal colloquialisms and local dialect are difficult to comprehend, but the people are friendly and more welcoming than in Edinburgh. 'You'll already have eaten dinner' – instead of the abrupt Edinburgh comment, a Glaswegian will be more likely invite you for dinner.

EDINBURGH

MAP INSIDE BACK COVER
When people think of Edinburgh (126 D6) *(∅ K–L12)* **they probably think of countless festivals, bagpipes and Dr Jekyll and Mr Hyde. Since the new millennium heralded a revival of the city's reputation, the New Town area especially radiates a contemporary and chic atmosphere.**

Photo: The Dugald Stewart Monument on Calton Hill in Edinburgh

Majestic and welcoming: Scotland's metropolises are growing closer together

CITY **WHERE TO START?**

Waverley Station: the city's main station is within easy walking distance of the Old Town where you can visit the Royal Mile, New Town and Princes Street. The airport bus also stops at this station. For parking it is recommended to head straight to Waverley, the Castle or St James shopping centre in New Town.

Even though Edinburgh is smaller than Glasgow, Scotland's capital sets the country's pace in every respect – not only when it comes to politics. Aside from its famous festivals, Edinburgh boasts a revamped port, boutique hotels, stylish clubs, exclusive shopping emporiums, restaurants with Michelin star cuisine and the remarkable new houses of parliament, which had a final cost of £430 million, right in the middle of its historical centre – now a World Heritage Site. Edinburgh's skyline is highlighted by the dramatic *Edinburgh Castle* perched up high like a crown, overlooking the city. Spread out directly below it is *Old Town*, the historic centre of Edinburgh with its winding alleys, pubs and tall, narrow 16th and 17th century

A step back in time:
Dean Village on the River Leith

buildings once frequented by the likes of Sir Walter Scott, philosopher David Hume and painter Henry Raeburn. After Edinburgh avoided bankruptcy following the union with England in 1707, it flourished financially and intellectually. The building of nearby New Town established a spacious central area. The Georgian architecture is characterised by wide streets and attractive squares as well as smart shops. Grim inner-city over there, and metropolitan flair over here – the city has two souls. This has inspired plenty of festivals and literary triumphs. The writers Ian Rankin ('Inspector Rebus') and

Irvine Welch ('Trainspotting') evoke the dark side, while Joanne K. Rowling ('Harry Potter') hails the magical side. Writing has always been a tradition in this city: Robert Burns, Sir Walter Scott and Robert Louis Stevenson all left their mark not only in the exhibits at the *Writers' Museum.* The narrative tradition and love for it, is continued today at the INSIDER TIP *The Scottish Storytelling Centre* (Mon–Sat 10am–6pm | 43 High Street | www.scottishstorytellingcentre. co.uk) in *John Knox House* with its fascinating exhibits and readings. Every year in August Edinburgh reminds its citizens and visitors alike of its special relationship with literature when it celebrates the *Book Festival (www.edbookfest.co.uk)* where numerous well-known authors take centre stage.

Edinburgh also has a say again when it comes to politics. For almost three centuries, the city was insignificant when it came to political affairs, but all that changed in 1999. The newly elected MSPs (members of parliament) created the new Scottish Parliament. So much atmosphere, drive and literary talent must be celebrated. Not only in August, throughout the year is a festival season for science, theatre, literature, cycling and more.

SIGHTSEEING

CALTON HILL ● 🌿 (U E3) (*m e3*)
The two best views of the city are east of Edinburgh city centre. The green *Calton Hill* is the lower one at 100 m/328 ft and is littered with grandiose monuments from the first half of the 19th century such as the unfinished war memorial, the *National Monument.*

Some 2 km/1.2 mi beyond Holyrood and the Scottish Parliament is the 251 m/823 ft high *Arthur's Seat.* A hill that is actually the basalt core of a 350 million year old volcano. The steep climb gives you stunning views of the parliament buildings and west over the cityscape.

EDINBURGH CASTLE ★ (U C4) (𝄞 c4)

A trip to Edinburgh would not be complete without a visit to the castle. Its chapel dates as far back as the 12th century, its main building is from the 18th and 19th century and its walls contain the *Scottish National War Museum,* the Scottish crown jewels and the *Stone of Destiny* – used in the coronation ceremonies of the Scottish monarchs.

In August, the castle becomes the focal point of the *Military Tattoo (www.edintattoo.co.uk),* opening with a military parade at the castle and culminating in a massive street festival. *April–Sept daily 9.30am– 6pm, Oct–March 9.30am–5pm | £17 | Castlehill | www.edinburghcastle.gov.uk*

GREYFRIARS KIRKYARD ●
(U D5) (𝄞 d5)

Just inside the gate of this cemetery is the statue of a Skye terrier called Bobby. Legend has it that after his master was buried here in 1858 the loyal dog spent the next 14 years guarding his grave. Take a guided tour to hear stories like the 'Greyfriars Bobby' as well as those of William Burke and William Hare. They were two men who dug up freshly buried bodies to sell to Edinburgh's Institute of Anatomical Research. When demand exceeded supply they gave in to temptation and the two men became serial killers. They murdered at least 16 people before they were caught. *Chambers Street/Candlemaker Row*

LEITH RIVER (0)

You don't trust the urban lady to do rural charm? Then take a walk along the

---

★ **Edinburgh Castle**
Fascinating landmarks at the majestic castle are the chapel and Stone of Destiny → **p. 45**

★ **Royal Botanic Garden**
For genuine regal breaks from Edinburgh's hustle and bustle: a green oasis beneath Victorian glass → **p. 47**

★ **Royal Mile**
Writer Daniel Defoe called it 'the finest street in the world' → **p. 47**

★ **The Scottish Parliament**
An outstanding and bold architectural homage to the city and country → **p. 47**

★ **Restaurant Martin Wishart**
The Scot is a chef in Edinburgh who cooks food fit for kings → **p. 48**

★ **Rosslyn Chapel**
A must-see since Dan Brown's 'The Da Vinci Code': the chapel with the mysterious stone carvings → **p. 51**

★ **Glasgow School of Art**
Visit upcoming artists at Mackintosh's art nouveau site → **p. 53**

★ **Kelvingrove Park**
The city park with river, university and museums outshines Glasgow's green spaces → **p. 53**

★ **Bute**
Glasgow's island retreat with Mount Stuart House → **p. 58**

★ **Hill House**
Built and styled – down to the last detail – by Mackintosh → **p. 58**

MARCO POLO HIGHLIGHTS

National Museum: from the café, you cannot only admire the Victorian glass roof

River Leith through Stockbridge and Dean Village. The river flows through a green canyon – a **INSIDER TIP** superb jogging route – and a short climb up gets you to an unexpected art haven: the *Scottish National Gallery of Modern Art One* and *Modern Art Two* exhibit works from the 19th century to present day, the latter is also home to the works of Eduardo Paolozzi, Edinburgh's top artist. Next to the galleries is *Dean Cemetery* in full grandeur. *Galleries daily 10am–5pm | admission free | 75 Belford Road | www. nationalgalleries.org*

NATIONAL GALLERIES OF SCOTLAND
(U C4) (ℳ c4)

Whatever art period inspires you, Edinburgh is bound to have the appropriate gallery. The *National Gallery of Scotland*, a neo-Classical bastion of art from 1859, is ideally located between Old Town and New Town. Inside you will find the history of painting on its crowded walls – from Holbein to Goya and Van Gogh to Cézanne. Connected to the gallery is

the more modern *Royal Scottish Academy Building* showing special exhibitions. January is the only month that the curators put the **INSIDER TIP** highly sensitive William Turner watercolours on display – the rest of the year they are locked away to save them from exposure to daylight. *Daily 10am–5pm, Thu until 7pm | admission free | The Mound | www.national galleries.org*

NATIONAL MUSEUM OF SCOTLAND
(U D5) (ℳ d5)

The convex new sandstone façade opposite the somewhat mysterious *Greyfriars Kirkyard* is a strong statement of modern-day Scotland. Inside, Scotland is presented in a contemporary way that goes beyond the clichés – everything from witches and relics to information about Dolly the cloned sheep. The ✦ *Tower Restaurant (daily noon–11pm | tel. 0131 2 25 30 03 | www.towerrestaurant.com | Moderate)* has spectacular views of the city. *Daily 10am–5pm | admission free | Chambers Street | www.nms.ac.uk*

NEW TOWN
(U B–D 2–4) *(ᗰ b–d 2–4)*

In about 1800, severe overcrowding caused the building of a new, ultra-chic inner city area with its typical Georgian architecture. Nowadays, this means that Edinburgh's centre with its tram route along the main Princes Street has two old towns on each side. Don't miss the walk along the main George Street, between Charlotte Square with the government buildings and St Andrew Square with the luxury department store Harvey Nichols. 19th-century architecture was never as appealing and sophisticated as between the districts of Broughton and Stockbridge.

PALACE OF HOLYROODHOUSE
(U F4) *(ᗰ f4)*

'Queenie's timeshare' is what the locals jokingly call it. The queen does indeed only spend one week a year in her official residence in Scotland. An abbey in the 12th century, it became the royal seat 400 years later. Robert Louis Stevenson wrote, 'Holyrood is a house of many memories. Wars have been plotted, dancing has lasted deep into the night, murder has been done in its chambers.' *April–Oct daily 9.30am–6pm, Nov–March 9.30am–4.30pm | £12.50 | Canongate | www.royalcollection.org.uk*

ROYAL BOTANIC GARDEN ★
(U B1) *(ᗰ b1)*

The Victorian Palm House (£5.50) – the largest in the United Kingdom – is its focal point. It houses 2400 species of 5400 plants and has ongoing exhibitions like that of Scottish artist, philosopher and landscaper Ian Hamilton Finlay. *Nov–Jan daily 10am–4pm, Feb/Oct 10am–5pm, March–Sept 10am–6pm | admission free | Arboretum Place | www.rbge.org.uk*

ROYAL MILE ★ ● (U C3–F4) *(ᗰ c3–f4)*

This is probably the world's most dramatic historic street: in the 18th century some 60,000 people lived along the Mile in buildings that were up to 15 floors high. Lawyers, prostitutes, wealthy citizens and poor men alike made their way through its filth and sewage, while the likes of philosopher David Hume and poet Robert Ferguson – whose statues adorn the route – would ponder the dire state of affairs. History is in evidence everywhere here including the home of Calvinist reformer John Knox who clashed with fun-loving Catholic Mary Queen of Scots. Look out for the pub that bears Deacon Brodie's name, an Edinburgh citizen whose double life inspired author Robert Louis Stevenson's novel 'Dr Jekyll and Mr Hyde'.

Today thousands upon thousands of visitors make their way across its old cobbled pavements leading downhill from Castle Hill to the Palace of Holyrood via High Street on to Canongate. Along the way are all things Scottish: kilts, whisky, bagpipes, oatmeal biscuits and – on a guided tour – scary anecdotes *(→ p. 110)*. *www.royal-mile.com*

ROYAL YACHT BRITANNIA
(131 D6) *(ᗰ L12)*

Even Margaret Rutherford, the 'Miss Marple' actress, has been on board. After almost 50 years in service the Britannia is now anchored on the River Leith. An audio tour accompanies a visit through its five decks. *Jan–March, Nov/Dec daily 10am–3.30pm, April–Sept daily 9.30am–4.30pm, Oct 9.30am–4pm | £15.50 | Ocean Terminal Leith | www.royalyachtbritannia.co.uk*

THE SCOTTISH PARLIAMENT ★
(U F4) *(ᗰ f4)*

After its opening in 2004 the highly controversial parliamentary building now has record numbers of visitors. Its poetic modern architecture integrates elements of the Scottish countryside with Edinburgh's distinctive old alleyways in an ingenious and unobtrusive way. Free access to the public areas. *Daily 10am–5pm (closed in Feb); Mon–Sat one-hour, free guided tours | audio guides can be reserved, guides can be downloaded for smartphone and tablets | Canongate | tel. 0131 3 48 52 00 | www.parliament.scot*

ST GILES CATHEDRAL (U D4) (*m̃ d4*)

The compact Mother Church of Scottish Presbyterianism is prominent on the Royal Mile. The columns in its sanctuary date back to 1120 and are its oldest architectural relics. When the English destroyed the church, it was rebuilt in the Gothic architectural style, providing the perfect stage for the inflammatory sermons of reformer John Knox (1514–72) who preached at the church for twelve years. The chapel of the Scottish Order of the Thistle, added in 1911, is a real treasure chest of exquisite woodwork and carved masonry. The Queen, as Sovereign, and her offspring Prince Charles and Princess Anne are members and bring up the number of 16 knights to the total of 19. Each Thistle knight has their own seat decorated with their coats of arms. Commoners have to have one designed before they can be admitted to the Order and are then seated in the stalls. While some of the knights' statues look quite bizarre, the cathedral's most curious treasure has to be that of two angels playing the bagpipes. Enjoy a unique panoramic view INSIDER TIP during a guided tour of the church tower (£6) for small groups. *May–Sept Mon–Fri 9am–7pm, Sat 9am–5pm, Oct–April Mon–Sat 9am–5pm, every Sun 1pm–5pm | Royal Mile/Lawnmarket | admission free | www.stgilescathedral.org.uk*

FOOD & DRINK

THE DOGS (U C3) (*m̃ c3*)

Wacky New Town vibe with kitsch and arty dog theme décor. Cheap, simple, and good food, cosy and often full. *Daily | 110 Hanover Street | tel. 0131 2 20 12 08 | www.thedogsonline.co.uk | Budget*

THE GRAIN STORE
(U D5) (*m̃ d5*)

The atmosphere inside its old stone walls and cool and attentive service makes it deserve five stars. Excellent food for reasonable prices – as has now been the case for more than 20 years. The kitchen even manages to refine black pudding. *Daily | 30 Victoria Street | tel. 0131 2 25 76 35 | www.grainstore-restaurant.co.uk | Moderate*

KYLOE RESTAURANT & GRILL
(U B4) (*m̃ b4*)

Located at the foot of the castle in the West End is the city's new favourite restaurant in the Rutland Hotel. Its food and wine are top class and there are some great window seats or secluded nooks for a romantic dinner. *Daily | 1–3 Rutland Street | tel. 0131 2 29 34 02 | www.kyloerestaurant.com | Moderate*

OLIVE BRANCH (U D2) (*m̃ d2*)

In Broughton, the neighbourhood with a strong gay scene. Colourful bunch of people, generous portions of mostly fried or deep-fried foods and good Sunday brunch. *Daily | 91 Broughton Street | tel. 0131 5 57 85 89 | www.theolivebranchscotland.co.uk | Moderate*

RESTAURANT MARTIN WISHART ★ (0)

Holding on to his Michelin star since 2001. His cuisine is rated as the best in Edinburgh, if not in Scotland. Pleasant, simple interior! *Closed Sun/Mon | 54 The Shore | tel. 0131 5 53 35 57 | www.restaurantmartinwishart.co.uk | Expensive*

SHOPPING

New Town's most fashionable street would have to be *George Street* (U B–C 3–3) *(⌂ b–c 3–4)*. Here row upon row of dignified building façades invite window shoppers and shoppers alike. At its most eastern end is the newly refurbished St Andrew's Square (U D3) *(⌂ d3)*. *Harvey Nichols* opened its exclusive department store here and has drawn other luxury brands into the area – especially to *Multrees Walk (www.the-walk.co.uk)*. If delightfully eccentric clothing and recycled fashions are your thing, then *Joey D (www.joey-d.co.uk)* in Broughton Street (U D2) *(⌂ d2)* is just the place for you. Why not take home one of their outlandish and unconventional handbags.

Princes Street (U B–D4) *(⌂ b–d4)* divides your shopping excursion into a New Town and Old Town experience. You'll find shop upon shop in the northern stretch of this boulevard with the southern stretch opening up to the fantastic skyline of Old Town and to the *Princes Street Gardens* – the best spot to relax after you've done all your shopping. Princes Street is also where you'll find the labyrinth of shops that make up the traditional department store *Jenners. Cockburn Street* (U D4) *(⌂ d4)* is for music fans with its well-stocked shops. Now that you've reached Old Town, look out for whisky and tartan in the Royal Mile shops. Even more exciting are the concentration of small independent shops surrounding Grassmarket and Victoria Street – terrific fashion, second-hand kilts, imaginative hats, modern knitwear and more (U C–D5) *(⌂ c–d5)*.

ENTERTAINMENT

CAFÉ ROYAL CIRCLE BAR
(U D3) *(⌂ d3)*
This pub has impressive and opulent Victorian interior and tile art dating back to 1886. Adjoining it is a good seafood restaurant. *19 West Register Street | www.caferoyaledinburgh.co.uk*

In good weather, the pub bar extends outdoors

GEORGE STREET
(U B–C 3–4) *(⌂ b–c 3–4)*
This exclusive Edinburgh area also has the coolest cocktail bars such as *Opal Lounge (no. 51)*, *Tigerlily (no. 125)* and *Rick's (55a Frederick Street)*. If you prefer less hustle and bustle try the *Outhouse (12 Broughton Street Lane)* in the relaxed Broughton neighbourhood.

LEITH (0)
The old harbour area of Leith has evolved into a popular part of the city for Michelin-quality eating and drinking. There

are also the tried and trusted gastropubs offering good culinary fare such as *King's Wark (36 The Shore)* and the atmospheric bistro-bar *The Shore (3 The Shore)* with its harbour view.

SANDY BELLS ● (U D5) (*m d5*)
Some of the city's best folk musicians frequent this unpretentious music pub for a beer, enriching the evening jam sessions with the sounds of their fiddles and accordions. *Daily | 25 Forrest Road*

THE VOODOO ROOMS (U D3) (*m d3*)
Right above the Café Royal Bar are several bars and salons with cool interiors known as Voodoo Rooms. The food is outstanding. Afterwards, you can enjoy drinks in the bars or enjoy the latest live bands. *19a West Register Street | www. thevoodoorooms.com*

WHERE TO STAY

ANGEL'S SHARE HOTEL (U B4) (*m b4*)
Cool, urban hotel with modern rooms in the West End district. A premier location between the Old Town, New Town and Dean Village. *Tram connection to the airport. 30 rooms | 9–11 Hope Street | tel. 0131 2 47 70 00 | www.angelssharehotel. com | Moderate*

THE BALMORAL (U C4) (*m c4*)
A home away from home to the stars, this palatial building with its clock tower stands out on the eastern end of Princes Street. Its luxury extends to its spa and the restaurants, *Number One* (Michelin star) and *Hadrian's*. It all comes at a price of course. *188 rooms | 1 Princes Street | tel. 0131 5 56 24 14 | short.travel/scot16 | Expensive*

GRASSMARKET HOTEL (U C5) (*m c5*)
Below the castle, at the heart of the busiest square in the Old Town area, you can relax in snug rooms decorated with fresh, youthful themes and modern facilities. *45 rooms | 94–96 Grassmarket | tel. 0131 2 20 22 99 | www.thegrassmarket hotel.co.uk | Moderate*

HOTEL DU VIN (U D5) (*m d5*)
A boutique hotel in an Old Town building with a superb bistro restaurant and fine rooms. Plus: cigar lounge, wine bar and whisky tasting room (reservations essential). The building was once an asylum and the poet Robert Fergusson died here at the age of 24. *47 rooms | 11 Bristo Place | tel. 0131 2 85 14 79 | www. hotelduvin.com | Moderate–Expensive*

MALMAISON (O)
One of the city's older designer hotels, charming atmosphere. *100 rooms | 1 Tower Place | Leith | tel. 0131 4 68 50 00 | www. malmaison.com | Moderate–Expensive*

SHERATON GRAND HOTEL ●
(U B5) (*m b5*)
A genuine upstart of all the centrally located hotels. Its 1980s decor blends with simple chic and its more expensive rooms overlook the castle. It boasts the best spa in the capital (also for non-residents). In addition to the usual fitness classes, treatments using hot stones and ayurvedic techniques are also offered, as are facials, manicures and massages. The superb swimming pool stretches right to the edge of the roof. *269 rooms | 1 Festival Square | tel. 0131 2 21 77 77 | www. sheratonedinburgh.co.uk | www.onespa. com | Expensive*

INFORMATION

EDINBURGH ICENTRE (U C4) (*m c4*)
3 Princes Street | tel. 0131 4 73 38 68 (*) | www.edinburgh.org

Famous from the film and TV: Rosslyn Chapel, the setting for Dan Brown's 'The Da Vinci Code'

WHERE TO GO

THE FORTH RAIL BRIDGE
(130 C6) *(𝄞 K12)*

A true landmark completed in 1890 it spans the Firth of Forth with its grandiose timber framework trusses and 6.5 million steel rivets. Take the train from Waverley to Dalmeny. *www.the forthbridges.org | 20 km/12.4 mi west of Edinburgh*

LINLITHGOW PALACE (126 C1) *(𝄞 K12)*

Documented for the first time in 1301, Linlithgow Palace was the birthplace of Mary, Queen of Scots. The picturesque castle ruins are in a park. *April–Sept daily 9.30am–5.30pm, Oct–March 10am–4pm | £5.50 | www.historicenvironment.scot | M9 | 25 km/15.5 mi west of Edinburgh*

ROSSLYN CHAPEL ★ (127 D2) *(𝄞 L13)*

The 15th-century Gothic chapel is the setting for the dramatic final scenes of the film thriller based on Dan Brown's novel 'The Da Vinci Code', and a lot of fans visit the site. Centre of attention is the *Apprentice Pillar* and some mysterious stone carvings – possibly encoded musical scores. In 2007 the musician Stuart Mitchell translated these into 'The Rosslyn Motet'. *Mon–Sat 9.30am–6pm, Sun noon–4.45pm | £9 | www.rosslynchapel. org.uk | 12 km/7.5 mi south of Edinburgh*

Glasgow School of Art: an inspirational setting for upcoming fashion designers

GLASGOW

MAP ON PAGES 138/139
(125 E–F 1–2) (𝔐 J13) Things are traditionally larger than life here. Glasgow will give you a down-to-earth and warm welcome. You discover amazing architecture alongside the charm of crumbling buildings; this is fertile ground for contemporary artists and an electrifying music scene as well as the crazy football antics of top clubs Celtic and Rangers. Glasgow was a thriving city when the River Clyde became a navigable waterway about two centuries ago. It became colonial Britain's second richest trading port. After the depression due to the rapid industrial decline, since the early 1990s the city has recovered. Nowadays, the ancestors of Catholic Irish families and Protestant Highlanders live in a city whose identity is based on its cultural offers, its appeal to students and its trendy art scene. They embrace the slogan that Glasgow was previously selling merchandise to the world and now marketing itself. This earned Glasgow the accolade of European City of Culture (1990), UK City of Architecture and Design (1999), Unesco City of Music (2008) and as the venue for the Commonwealth Games (2014).

The area around Buchanan Street is regarded as Scotland's best shopping area, the promenade along the previously industrialised River Clyde is now a fabulous pedestrian precinct. Classical and Victorian buildings are attractive. The buildings especially designed a century ago by the aesthete and art nouveau designer Charles Rennie Mackintosh lure visitors to tour Glasgow's architecture. It is hoped that the famous Glasgow School of Art, which has trained generations of avantgarde artists, will be rebuilt after another recent devastating fire.

The nightlife with live music is another top attraction and for many years has

---

WHERE TO START?

George Square: From the square at Queen Street railway station everything is within easy walking distance. You can reach the University of Glasgow, the School of Art and Kelvingrove Park via Buchanan and Sauchiehall Streets. The River Clyde lies south of the park. There are car parks on George Square, St Enoch Shopping Centre and at the Clyde Auditorium (known as the 'Armadillo') on the River Clyde.

attracted brilliant musicians to Glasgow like Jack Bruce (Cream), Alex Kapranos (Franz Ferdinand), Amy Macdonald, Belle & Sebastian, Roddy Frame (Aztec Camera), Glasvegas or since 2010 the INSIDER TIP Electronica and jazz musicians of Hidden Orchestra.

SIGHTSEEING

CENTRE FOR CONTEMPORARY ARTS CCA (139 D2)

From spoken word performance to landscaping: just about any form of contemporary art can be practised and showcased here. The focus is on the fine arts, film, music, dance and performances – but even if you're simply after a cup of coffee you will still be welcome. *Tue–Sat 11am–6pm | 350 Sauchiehall Street | www.cca-glasgow.com*

GEORGE SQUARE (139 F3–4)

Glasgow's central square is surrounded by statues of poets, politicians and royalty. It is a popular spot for locals to relax at lunchtime. The square is dominated by the *City Chambers* – headquarters of the Glasgow City Council. Built of Scottish granite and Italian marble it is well worth a visit. On a street corner south of here is *Merchant City (www. merchantsquareglasgow.com)* between Ingram Street and Tron Gate, a hip area with lovely cafés, restaurants and boutiques – meeting place of the young business and design scene.

GLASGOW SCHOOL OF ART ★ (139 D2)

Built by Charles Rennie Mackintosh in 1896, and situated high above the city, the art school is considered as the British temple for young artists. Unfortunately, due to a fire in mid-2014 – and a further devastating fire in June 2018 – Glasgow's

architectural landmark is closed until further notice. Sadly, the famous art nouveau library was already destroyed in 2014. *167 Renfrew Street | www.gsa.ac.uk*

GLASGOW SCIENCE CENTRE ● (0)

The centre offers educational insights into complex scientific matters and is suitable for children. It has an Imax cinema and the 127-m/417-ft high ☆ *Glasgow Tower* with an overview of the Clydebank that sways in the wind. Opposite, the Science Centre and Clyde Auditorium (nicknamed 'Armadillo') gleam like overturned barrels with their metal frames – their cool modernist design is a notable feature of the city's versatile architecture. Walk across the Clyde Walkway, starting at Glasgow Green Park. *March–Oct daily 10am–5pm, Nov–Feb Mon, closed Tue | £11, Glasgow Tower only £5.50 | 50 Pacific Quay | www.glasgowsciencecentre.org*

HUNTERIAN MUSEUM AND ART GALLERY (138 A1)

Geological, archaeological and historical collections as well as art treasures and the outstanding *Mackintosh House* – a reconstruction of Charles Rennie Mackintosh's studio. *Tue–Sat 10am–5pm, Sun 11am–4pm | admission free | University Avenue | Kelvingrove | www.hunterian.gla.ac.uk*

KELVINGROVE ART GALLERY & MUSEUM ● (138 A1–2)

The red sandstone building is a tourist magnet with natural science exhibits and a contemporary view of Scottish life. *Mon–Tue, Sat 10am–5pm, Fri/Sun 11am–5pm | admission free | Argyle Street | Kelvingrove*

KELVINGROVE PARK ★ (138 A–B 1–2)

The most beautiful of the city's 70 or so parks. The small Kelvin River meanders

Breathe in the fresh air:
time for a break in Kelvingrove Park

past the *Kelvingrove Art Gallery & Museum*, the *Hunterian Museum* and the Victorian baroque building of the *University of Glasgow* built in 1864. East of the park's border are houses designed by architect Charles Wilson in 1854 for well-to-do Glaswegians. If you feel like a pleasant walk: explore the Kelvin 10 km/6.2 mi westwards out of town. *Kelvin Way/off Kelvin Bridge*

THE LIGHTHOUSE ✺ (139 E4)

A lighthouse for Mackintosh! Designed by the master architect himself in 1895 for the "Glasgow Herald" newspaper, it now houses the Scotland Centre for Architecture, Design and the City. The tower has excellent views of the city and a design shop, exhibitions, a Mackintosh information centre and a café. *Mon–Sat 10.30am–5pm, Sun noon–5pm | admis-*

sion free | 11 Mitchell Lane | www.thelighthouse.co.uk

NECROPOLIS ● ✺ (0)

There are uninterrupted views of the city from this expansive hill-top cemetery near Glasgow's cathedral. Walk around the cemetery and you'll get a perspective on how the citizens of the city's Victorian era were buried with Gothic and neo-Classical monuments and sculptures, including the obelisk to the strict Anglican preacher John Knox. *Main entrance: 70 Cathedral Square*

PEOPLE'S PALACE (0)

Opened in 1898, the city's turbulent social history is on display here in this domed building. Relax with a cup of tea beneath palm trees. *Tue–Thu, Sat 10am–5pm, Fri/Sun 11am–5pm | admission free | Glasgow Green East End*

RIVERSIDE MUSEUM (0)

Architectural talking point and Waterfront Renewal Project. The spectacular museum located on the banks of the Clyde River replaced the old transport museum on the Kelvin in 2011. The design by Zaha Hadid Architects cleverly incorporated the ship building industry into the building. Steam engines, racing cars and all things transport related are on display. In front of the building is the steel-hulled Glenlee (1896) while on the opposite bank is the Govan shipyard which is building two aircraft carriers. *Mon–Thu, Sat 10am–5pm, Fri/Sun 11am–5pm | admission free | Pointhouse Place | www.glasgowlife.org.uk/museums*

FOOD & DRINK

CORINTHIAN (139 F4)

Centrally located in Merchant City, serving inspired fusion cuisine in an atmosphere of elegance and urban ease. Go there for lunch at least. *Daily | 191 Ingram Street | tel. 0141 5 52 11 01 | www.thecorinthianclub.co.uk | Moderate–Expensive*

CRABBSHAKK (138 A2)

Cosy, cabin charm on three floors. Seafood galore served: treat yourself to oysters and champagne and fish and chips served in style. *Daily | 1114 Argyle Street | tel. 0141 3 34 61 27 | www.crabshakk.com | Moderate*

GANDOLFI FISH (139 F4)

This elegant restaurant serves seafood from the Hebrides, which is also where head chef Jamie Donald hails from. A few doors further on is *Café Gandolfi (64 Albion Street | tel. 0141 5 52 68 13 | Budget)* a culinary institution – it has been going strong for 30 years – with a charming bar. *Daily | 84–86 Albion Street | tel. 0141 5 52 94 75 | www.gandolfifish.com | Moderate*

MOTHER INDIA (138 A2)

Possibly the best Indian restaurant north of London. Indian beer is served with the fragrant ingredients. Or take along your own bottle of wine. *Daily | 28 Westminster Terrace | tel. 0141 2 21 16 63 | Budget*

THE UBIQUITOUS CHIP (0)

This restaurant is as Scottish as it gets and they also note where their fish, beef or dessert ingredients have been sourced from. A less pricy option is the bistro *(Budget)* upstairs. *Daily | 12 Ashton Lane | tel. 0141 3 34 50 07 | www.ubiquitouschip.co.uk | Moderate–Expensive*

SHOPPING

Glasgow has deservedly earned its reputation alongside London as Britain's best shopping area. The sandstone buildings of *Buchanan Street* offer everything that is synonymous with elegant shopping. All the top designers are represented at the luxury mall *Princes Square (48 Buchanan Street)*, while around the corner in *Ingram Street* are some luxury brands such as *Mulberry*. Trendy design stores have moved into the sandstone buildings at *Merchant City* between Ingram Street and Trongate. If you like creative student shops and quirky designer stores, explore the area around *Byres Road*, west of the university. *Pink Poodle (no. 181–183)* sells fun modern attire, *Vintage Guru (no. 195)* and *Starry Starry Night (19–21 Downside Lane)* are packed with vintage clothing. It's also worth visiting the boutiques in the *Italian Centre (7 John Street)* and at *St Enoch Centre* on the same square.

LOW BUDGET

Do you know how much you are willing to spend on dinner? Then simply place your bid at *www.priceyourmeal.com* where you can secure a seat at a restaurant in Glasgow or Edinburgh.

Cheap rates for accomodation can be found on the website of the Glasgow City Marketing Bureau: *peoplemakeglasgow.com*.

Tip for Edinburgh: *The Halfway House pub (daily | 24 Fleshmarket Close)* is tucked away between the Royal Mile and the railway station up a steep, narrow alley. Offering delicious traditional, home-made food, good beer and warm atmosphere.

ENTERTAINMENT

THE ARCHES (139 E4)
There is always something on offer in The Arches beneath Glasgow Central railway station. A bar, arts venue and theatre and night club will leave you spoilt for choice with their repertoire of gigs and events. Top-notch sound. *253 Argyle Street | tel. 0141 2 21 40 01 | www.thearches.co.uk*

BEN NEVIS (138 A2)
Celtic-style local pub in the West End. The owner is from the Highlands and has decorated his whisky emporium (180 types!) in the traditional style. For a Scotch at its Scottish best! *Daily | 1197 Argyle Street*

KING TUT'S WAH WAH HUT (139 D3)
Sweaty walls and on trend music, this is the UK's top address for the club scene. To make it as a band you have to have a gig here. *Daily | 272a St Vincent Street | tel. 0141 2 21 52 79 | www.kingtuts.co.uk*

NICE 'N' SLEAZY (139 D2)
Big burgers (*Budget*) and cool jukebox music, live gigs and hip dance floor. *Daily | 421 Sauchiehall Street | tel. 0141 3 33 96 37 | www.nicensleazy.com*

ORAN MOR (0)
This converted parish church is now a multi-purpose venue and behind its façades are two restaurants, two bars and a nightclub. The auditorium is magnificent and will make you feel a little closer to the heavens. *Daily | Byres Road/Great Western Road | tel. 0141 3 57 62 26 | www.oran-mor.co.uk*

INSIDER TIP SCOTIA BAR (139 F5)
In Glasgow's oldest pub there is a real buzz with poetry slams, blues and rock and swearing. It's crazy! Opposite is the equally famous and atmospheric *Clutha Vaults*, where a helicopter crashed in 2013, and killed ten guests. Scotland's leader attended the reopening and served pints. *Daily | 112 Stockwell Street | tel. 0141 5 52 86 81*

WHERE TO STAY

BABBITY BOWSTER (0)
Popular rooms in one of the Scottish city pubs. A top location in Merchant City, so booking is essential! *5 rooms | 16–18 Blackfriars Street | tel. 0141 5 52 50 55 | Budget*

CITIZEN M (139 E2)
Reasonably priced, urban, well-designed chic. Plenty of space for chillaxing. *198 rooms | 60 Renfrew Street | tel. 0141 4 04 94 85 | www.citizen.com | Budget*

HILTON GARDEN INN (139 F4)
The large hotel benefits from its location on the River Clyde and the modern harbour atmosphere. Pleasant design. The rooms are small, but they have balconies. A terrace with excellent café and restaurant (*Budget*). *164 rooms | Finnieston Quay | tel. 0141 24 01 00 02 | www.placeshilton.com/glasgow-city-centre | Moderate*

MANOR PARK HOTEL (0)
The small terraced hotel in the West End has good parking facilities with a recreation park directly opposite. Excellent breakfast and welcoming Scottish hospitality. *10 rooms | 28 Belshagray Drive | tel. 0141 3 39 21 43 | www.themanorpark.com | Budget*

MERCHANT CITY INN (139 F4)
Simple but neat rooms in what used to be the home of a tobacco merchant, centrally located in Merchant City. No porter,

so be prepared to carry your suitcase up the stairs. *40 rooms | 52 Virginia Street | tel. 0141 5522424 | www.merchantcity inn.com | Budget*

MILLENNIUM HOTEL (139 F3)

This hotel probably boasts Glasgow's best location on the centrally situated George Square, right next to Queen Street Station. Breakfast is served in the winter-garden overlooking the hustle and bustle on the square; the spacious rooms are equipped with all the amenities for a city break. Typical Scottish cuisine in the Brasserie on George Square. *110 rooms | 40 George Square | tel. 0141 3326711 | www.millenniumhotels.co.uk/millenni-umglasgow | Moderate*

INFORMATION

GLASGOW ICENTRE (139 E4)

Gallery of Modern Art | Royal Exchange Square | tel. 0141 2044400 | people-makeglasgow.com

WHERE TO GO

ARRAN

(124–125 C–D 2–3) (🛲 G13–14)

This remote island is a miniature version of Scotland: it has mountains (the 874 m/2867 ft *Goat Fell*); standing stones on the Machrie Moor; a castle in *Brodick* town and a small, modern whisky distillery – its ten year old malt is one of the best. The best way to explore Arran is by hiring a bicycle. There are various activities available from sea kayaking to rock climbing *(www.arranadventure.com). Auchrannie Resort (85 rooms | tel. 01770 302234 | www.auchrannie.co.uk | Moderate) or Kilmichael House (7 rooms | tel. 01770 302219 | www.kilmichael.com | Expensive)* are two good accommodation options. Arran is also the perfect springboard to the distant Kintyre peninsula. *The car ferry from Ardrossan (25 km/15.5 mi west of Glasgow) to Brodick runs 6 times daily from Mon–Sat, the Lochranza–Claonaig (Kintyre) car ferry*

For individualists: off the beaten track the Isle of Arran is a miniature version of Scotland

Kintyre highlights: whisky and solitary Machrihanish beaches

9 times daily: Caledonian MacBrayne shipping company (tel. 01770 302166 | www.calmac.co.uk)

BUTE ★ (125 D1–2) (*𝑀 G13*)

This small island is in close proximity to Glasgow, it is a half hour train journey from Central Station to Wemyss Bay, followed by another half hour by ferry. After the introduction of the steam ship in the 19th century, *Rothesay* port became a popular weekend destination for well

heeled Glaswegians. However, in 1910 when holidays for the working classes were introduced, Rothesay lost its exclusivity. Make the *Victorian Toilets* at the harbour your first port of call — still in use today they are bound to make you smile. Next take a stroll through the town of Rothesay then head to the east coast's ● *Mount Stuart House (tours Easter and April–Oct daily noon–4pm | £11 | www.mountstuart.com).* The interior of the Gothic Revival red sandstone castle is the most esoteric and romantic in Scotland. Its last owner had a passion for Catholicism, astronomy and astrology — reflected in the magnificent marble chapel, the impressive entrance hall and the mythological detail in the rooms.

HILL HOUSE ★ (125 E1) (*𝑀 H12*)

An hour's drive from Glasgow, this house in Helensburgh was designed in detail by Charles Rennie Mackintosh and his wife. It was built in 1904 for publisher Walter Blackie and shows the Scottish art nouveau style with typical colours, wall hangings and décor. Also with tea garden, a library and a shop selling INSIDER TIP fun souvenirs by young Scottish designers: the ingredients for a perfect day out. *April–Oct daily 1.30pm–5.30pm | £10.50 | Upper Colquhoun Street | Helensburgh | 45 km/28 mi north-west of Glasgow*

HOLY ISLAND ● (125 D3) (*𝑀 G14*)

Some 1400 years ago a monk lived as a hermit on this island east of Arran. Monks are once again living on Holy Island after Buddhists arrived in the 1960s. Their monastery became famous despite its isolation: John Lennon, Leonard Cohen and David Bowie came here on a visit. The monastery is now a spiritual centre. Guests, including day visitors, are most welcome and can participate in meditation and prayers, even spend the night. *65 beds | tel. 01770 70 04 63 | www.holyisland.org | Budget*

(124 B–C 3–4) (*ɷ* F14)

The most south-westerly peninsula well off the beaten track and seldom included in tours, and this is despite the famous Paul McCartney song, 'Mull of Kintyre'. However, whisky connoisseurs come here to visit the three distilleries *Springbank (www.springbankwhisky.com), Glen Scotia (www.glenscotia.com)* and *Glengyle (www.kilkerransinglemalt.com).* Golfers also come here to try their hand at the *Machrihanish Golf Club* and its famously difficult first hole *(www.machgolf.com)* while nature lovers and hikers love the 8 km/5 mi *Machrihanish* beach from where you can see Ireland. *Approx. 200 km/124 mi west of Glasgow*

NEW LANARK (126 B3) (*ɷ* K13)

Robert Owen (1771–1858) was an industrialist and social reformer. The conditions in the cotton mills – while state-of-the art in his time – were crying out for reform. The industrial capitalists deployed children to operate the heavy machinery and they constituted 70 per cent of the labour force. It had become obvious to Owen that well treated, educated and healthy workers would mean higher profits. So, he improved their living conditions and increased the breaks of his 2500-strong operational workforce and also established a school and introduced health care and cultural activities in the workplace. His pioneering social model and the details and care with which he ran his organisation are documented in the New Lanark World Heritage site and museum. A good over night option is at the *Mill Hotel (38 rooms | tel. 01555 66 72 00 | Moderate)* built in an old spinning mill directly on the River Clyde. *April–Oct daily 10am–5pm, Nov–March daily 10am–4pm | £9.50 | www.newlanark.org | 50 km/31.1 mi south-east of Glasgow*

FOR BOOKWORMS AND FILM BUFFS

The Strange Case of Dr Jekyll and Mr Hyde – in his 1886 novel Robert Louis Stevenson indirectly criticises the hypocrisy of the Victorian era, its respectable outward appearance belying dark desires.

T 2-Trainspotting – Danny Boyle's second genius stroke about Renton, Begbie, Sick Boy and Spud, filmed in Edinburgh, 20 years after part 1 – this time based on themes in Irvine Welch's book 'Porno' – painfully reflects real life again. Only this time the wistfulness of growing old follows the youthful drug scene.

The Falls: an Inspector Rebus Novel – Edinburgh police detective John Rebus investigates a series of murders. The bodies of young women are found with a clue: a miniature coffin. Ian Rankin's dark and moody crime thrillers have attained cult status.

Outlander – Claire Randall was a nurse in the Second World War and – quick as a flash! – she steps inside a stone building in the Highlands and is back in the 18th century. The American TV series is based on the books by Diana Gabaldon. Stuff that the Highlands are made of!

THE HIGHLANDS

There is plenty going on in the Highlands with their mountains and heather moorlands. Only nine people live here per square mile, so there is lots of space for golf, deerstalking and hiking. And the enchanted atmosphere is thanks to the dramatic weather and Gaelic Highland spirit. Rising up directly behind Perth are the *Grampian Mountains*. A region that has become instrumental in shaping the popular image of Scotland: desolate and dramatic plateaus, heather and scattered sheep and majestic historic sites like *Glen Coe,* (the 'Valley of Tears') and legendary *Loch Ness*. While *Royal Deeside* in the east lures visitors with its castles and distilleries, the northern Highlands loom majestically, scattered with tiniest villages and a wild and rugged coastline.

ABERDEEN

(131 F1) (*N8*) **Because its granite stone gleams in the sunshine, Aberdeen, situated on the Don and Dee estuaries, is known as the 'Silver City by the Sea'. It is also Scotland's third largest city with a population of 230,000.**
Ranked behind Glasgow and Edinburgh it still leads a Cinderella existence even though its town privileges date way back to 1179. Today offshore oil has turned Aberdeen into Europe's oil capital. The city also attracted worldwide interest because of its granite. The local deposits of this silver-grey stone are one the world's best granite types. Aside from being used in housing construction in

Timeless myths and clichés: this is where Scottish men wear kilts and the Royal Family likes to spend annual holidays

Aberdeen, it has been used worldwide from the streets of London to the piers of Rio de Janeiro. In the 19th century its coastal location made shipbuilding an important economic factor in Aberdeen.

SIGHTSEEING

FOOTDEE
A fishing village that was built 200 years ago by the architect of Balmoral Castle, Footdee is on the coast where the River Dee flows into the sea. At the time the residents of Footdee (pronounced: Fittie) were fishermen but today it is home to a colourful mix of people and professions. This village-like outpost is about a half hour walk from Aberdeen city centre. The path leads along the busy Victoria Dock harbour with its huge warehouses, containers and silos. *Quay East*

MARISCHAL COLLEGE
The world's largest granite building was built here in 1837 for the university and you'd be forgiven for mistaking it for a

cathedral. It now houses the municipal offices. *Broad Street*

MARITIME MUSEUM
Exhibits about shipping, navigation and life on the oil platforms in a building from 1593. *Tue–Sat 10am–5pm, Sun 11.30am–5pm | admission free | Shiprow | www. aagm.co.uk*

ENTERTAINMENT

THE LEMON TREE
Raise the curtains for live excellent alternative performances. Opens just before the evening show. Try the local beer from Brewdog at the bar. *Daily | 5 West North Street | tel. 01224 64 11 22 | www. aberdeenperformingarts.com*

Marischal College: Aberdeen's neo-Gothic gem

FOOD & DRINK

FOOD STORY
Informal and quaint. The café prides itself on being Aberdeen's lounge for excellent vegetarian food. *Closed Sun | 13 Thistle Street | tel. 01224 62 22 93 | www.foodstory.co.uk | Budget*

SILVER DARLING
One of Scotland's best seafood restaurants is right here in Footdee, perched over the Dee estuary in what was once the outlook of the Aberdeen harbour pilot. *Closed Sun | tel. 01224 57 62 29 | www.thesilverdarling.co.uk | Expensive*

WHERE TO STAY

THE GLOBE INN
Let's turn up the volume! Cosy rooms above the pub that serves excellent food. Live music on weekends and theatre-goers cannot be ignored. *7 rooms | 13–15 North Silver Street | tel. 01224 62 42 58 | Moderate*

HILTON GARDEN INN
Modern, centrally located luxury hotel with some nice touches such as large rain showers, adjustable beds, a gym and a sumptuous breakfast. *110 rooms | 31 St Andrew Street | tel. 01224 45 14 44 | hiltongardeninn3.hilton.com | Moderate*

INFORMATION

ABERDEEN ICENTRE
23 Union Street | tel. 01224 90 04 90 | www.aberdeen-grampian.com

WHERE TO GO

BALLATER (131 D2) (*\U L8*)

This small Victorian village (population of 1500) lies 66 km/41 mi west of Aberdeen in the shadow of the Lochnagar Mountains. It has a close connection with the English royals as the Queen and her family spend their summer holidays at *Balmoral Castle (daily 10am–5pm | £12 | www.balmoralcastle. com)* only 10 km/6.2 mi away. As many of the shops supply Balmoral Castle they carry the Royal Warrant. Tourists can visit the castle, which is a fine example of Scots Baronial architecture, from May to July. The perfect place to stay is ● *Darroch Learg (12 rooms | Ballater (A 93) | tel. 01339 75 54 43 | www.darrochlearg. co.uk | Moderate)*. The country hotel and

restaurant, a picture-perfect establishment tucked away on a green hill, has comfortable, cosy rooms with four poster beds and decorations in tartan prints. The restaurant serves exquisite cuisine using local, seasonal produce.

BRAEMAR (130 C2) (*\U K8*)

The village is known for the *Highland Games* that take place on the first Saturday in September. Even the Queen, accompanied by the royal household, attends this traditional sports event that attracts some 20,000 spectators who descend on the tiny village (pop. 1200) annually – it is best to book early in the year *(info: tel. 0131 4 733 8 68 (*))!* 85 km/52.8 mi west of Aberdeen

CAIRNGORMS NATIONAL PARK (130–131 C–D 1–2) (*\U K 7–8*)

Great Britain's largest national park protects a quarter of the remaining Scottish forests and woodlands and many of its endangered plant species and wildlife. Balmoral Castle lies within its borders

---

⭐ **Ben Nevis**
A magnet for Munro climbers: Scotland's highest and most romantic mountain attracts many hikers and climbers to its summit → **p. 65**

⭐ **Glen Coe**
The 'Valley of Tears' reveals a tragic tale of betrayal and treachery – and it's an unforgettable outdoor experience → **p. 66**

⭐ **Cawdor Castle**
The place of Macbeth's trials: the wonderful castle setting for Shakespeare's tragic hero → **p. 68**

⭐ **Loch Ness**
Still as mysterious as the myths, legends and scare stories about its most famous resident: Nessie → **p. 70**

⭐ **Loch Lomond**
On the shores of Scotland's largest loch, the folk hero Rob Roy hid from his enemies. That's not the only reason his compatriots love the lake so much → **p. 71**

⭐ **Fife**
A peninsula with almost Mediterranean flair and the world's most famous golf club → **p. 72**

MARCO POLO HIGHLIGHTS

making it a favourite Royal Family holiday destination. Dominating the park are the 1300 m/4265 ft *Grampian Mountains*. A mountain road (A 939) wends its way through the barren, windy heights leading up to the Lecht ski resort *(www.lecht.co.uk)*. The park is popular with outdoor enthusiasts for its hiking and mountain bike trails (old paths once used by cattle drovers) as well as white river rafting (from Aviemore).

The River Dee, which flows into the sea at Aberdeen, has its source in the mountains here and *Royal Deeside* is what the Scots call the upper river valley. It encompasses the Balmoral estate where the royal family takes its vacation from August to October. If you take a walk in the park around that time you could even bump into nobility. You can join a Land Rover tour of the royal estate which gives visitors an idea of the efforts being made to boost the diminishing numbers of the magnificent Scottish pine. If you want to delve deeper into the secrets of Royal Deeside you should join the INSIDER TIP top rate tour that Ian Murray *(www.lochnagar.net)* conducts. He has documented the history of the area in four books. In addition to the historical tour, you can join a INSIDER TIP four-wheel drive through the mountains between Braemar and Ballater with former policeman Neil Bain *(www.braemarhighlandsafaris.co.uk)*. Even if you don't spot an eagle, deer or grouse; you will be entertained by his repertoire of funny anecdotes about the local farmers and whisky distillers. *www.visitcairngorms.*

CRATHES CASTLE (131 E2) *(M M8)*

Set in lush, landscaped gardens this is one of the most beautiful of Scotland's tower houses with magnificent interiors embellished with ceiling frescoes, antiques and one of the first holographs. The picture of a stag on the first floor ingeniously turns into a ship when you view it from the side. *April–Oct daily 10.30am–5pm, Jan–March, Nov/Dec Sat/Sun 11am–4pm | £12.50 | Banchory | 25 km/15.5 mi west of Aberdeen*

DUFFTOWN (135 D6) *(M L7)*

The village halfway between Inverness and Aberdeen with its seven distilleries is regarded as the capital not only of the whisky region in *Speyside*, but of the whisky world in general. It is surrounded by the *Malt Whisky Trail*, including one of the country's best whisky

BIRD DROPPINGS

If you get covered in bird droppings while bird watching, don't worry! You have probably ventured into a colony of nesting seabirds in early spring. For example, on Handa Island or Unst in Shetland. But it could be worse. If the arctic skua thinks its growing chicks are threatened in their grass nests, the brown gull will dive at your head and then its feet land on top! It's not much use falling to the ground – far better to try holding up the bird book. Things get messy in the breeding ground of arctic terns: they launch aerial attacks from all sides. But fulmars are the worst – they spit out their stomach contents. Otherwise, the Scots are generally friendly and hospitable!

shops (www.whiskyshopdufftown.co.uk) at the eye-catching clock tower in Dufftown. The Balvenie is one of the few

daily 9am–6pm, Nov–March daily 10am–5pm | £6 | www.dunnottarcastle.co.uk | 25 km/15.5 mi west of Aberdeen

Scotland's highest and most imposing mountain: Ben Nevis near Fort William

distilleries that produces its own barley malt thanks to floor malting and employs its own barrel makers. Hikers are recommended to try several stages of the 100-km/62-mi easily accessible and beautiful Speyside Way (www.speyside way.org) on the River. On the way from Dufftown to Grantown-on-Spey, you pass 18 distilleries. For accommodation and to sample the whisky – with 47 single malt barrels – try the Aberlour village pub Mash Tun (tel. 01340 88 17 71 | www.mashtun-aberlour.com | Moderate) – it's just a short walk from the similarly named distillery on the River Spey. 80 km/49.7 mi west of Aberdeen

DUNNOTTAR CASTLE (131 F2) (*M8*)

A dramatic and majestic castle ruin perched on a cliff overlooking the sea. A hiking trail leads up to it from the quaint, seaside town of Stonehaven. April–Oct

FORT WILLIAM

(129 E3) (*G10*) **If you are expecting a romantic Highlands town, Fort William (pop. 10,000) may come as a surprise.** The small town in the shadow of Ben Nevis mainly serves as a transport hub and transit station for tours to the Highlands. The town was established as a fortification in 1655 and has a small pedestrian zone that runs through it.

SIGHTSEEING

BEN NEVIS ★

The easy (but steep) hike up Great Britain's highest mountain (1344 m/ 4409 ft) is what draws visitors to Fort William in the summer (weather info:

www.bennevisweather.co.uk). At the foot of the mountain the Nevis meanders through the *Glen Nevis*, popular among mountain bikers, hikers and climbers for its cliffs, waterfalls and the wild, scenic countryside. The landscape looks like something straight out of a film, so it comes as no surprise that it was the back-

A wonderful bridge in Inverness

drop of choice for heroic epics such as 'Braveheart' and 'Rob Roy'. Experienced hikers will take a day or two to reach *Corrour Station (32 km/19.9 mi from Fort William)* in Rannoch Moor. A welcome sight as the Glasgow–Fort William line stops here on demand. 2 km/1.2 mi from the tiny train station building, on the fabulously beautiful *Loch Ossian*, is a ⊗ INSIDER TIP youth hostel *(Budget)* – off the grid and entirely reliant on wind and solar energy. www.glen-nevis.co.uk

FOOD & DRINK

CRANNOG AT THE WATERFRONT
One of your best options for fresh seafood. *Daily | Town Pier | tel. 01397 70 55 89 | www.crannog.net | Moderate*

WHERE TO STAY

THE LIME TREE
A Highland art gallery, an excellent restaurant and a small, newly renovated hotel all in one. *9 rooms | The Old Manse | Achintore Road | tel. 01397 70 18 06 | www. limetreefortwilliam.co.uk | Moderate*

INFORMATION

FORT WILLIAM ICENTRE
15 High Street | tel. 01397 70 18 01 | www. visit-fortwilliam.co.uk; www.lochaber.com

WHERE TO GO

GLEN COE ★ (129 E3) (𝑀 H10)
Steep and brooding cliff walls rise up on either side of the dramatic Glencoe Gorge which becomes more isolated as it leads up into the narrow valley. Also known as the 'Valley of Tears' it gets its name from a massacre that took place on 13 February 1692. The MacDonald clan chief was slow in pledging his oath of allegiance to King William of Orange. Wanting to set an example, the king used the Campbell's clan chief to carry out his plan. The latter stayed as a guest of the MacDonalds and during the night he and his men slaughtered the entire clan. This gruesome event is documented at the *Glencoe Visitor Centre (daily 10am–5pm | Glencoe (A82) | www.nts. org.uk)*. Also plenty information about the valley's hiking trails. *www.discover glencoe.scot | 26 km/15.2 mi south of Fort William*

INVERNESS

(134 A6) *(⟋ J 7)* **This lively city (pop. 72,000) is the primary city and shopping centre of the Highlands as well as being the hub for Highland and island tours.**

Capital of the Highlands, its landmark is the *Caledonian Canal* which joins the west coast with the east coast. The picturesque canal is also popular with houseboats and narrowboats and stretches over 90 km/55.9 mi with 29 locks.

RIVER NESS

This is where you should come if you are looking for some peace and quiet. The path takes you past suspension bridges towards the northern end of the Caledonian Canal. From Inverness to Fort William it is a stretch of 100 km/62 mi through the *Great Glen* with brilliant views of the canal along the way and of the Highland mountains on the horizon.

CASTLE RESTAURANT

Of course, Inverness has a castle and a restaurant. But it's more a simple café with homemade chips. Hearty Scottish, delicious cuisine. *Closed Sun | 41 Castle Street | tel. 01463 23 09 25 | Budget*

GIRVANS

On Sundays, you can enjoy an all-day breakfast. Excellent food and tempting cream cakes. *2 Stevens Brae | tel. 01463 71 19 00 | Budget*

THE RIVERHOUSE RESTAURANT

A famous fish restaurant, small, cosy and popular. Fresh mussels served on Wednesdays. *Closed Sun, Mon | 1 Greig Street | tel. 01463 22 20 33 | www.river houseinverness.co.uk | Moderate*

INVERBRORA FARM B&B

The typical robust Highland farmhouse is a modern home inside with cosy family atmosphere and very friendly hosts. Ideally located on the east coast halfway between Inverness (90 km/55.9 mi) and Thurso. *4 rooms | April–Sept | sign on A9, 1 km/0.6 mi south of Brora | tel. 01408 62 12 08 | www.inverbrora.com | Budget*

MOYNESS HOUSE

Victorian villa with some fun, fresh and friendly decorated rooms and excellent breakfast. Elegant B&B, 10 minutes from the centre. *7 rooms | 6 Bruce Gardens | tel. 01463 23 38 36 | www.moyness.co.uk | Moderate*

INVERNESS ICENTRE

Castle Wynd/Bridge Street | tel. 01463 25 24 01 | www.inverness-scotland.com

INSIDER TIP **ALLADALE LODGE** ◐
(134 A4) *(⟋ J7)*

Highlands deluxe: the lodge is set in a 23,000 acre private estate. The mountainous and isolated environment is great for excursions on foot, on horseback or by four-wheel drive vehicle – the lodge is also open to day visitors. The lodge accommodation *(7 rooms | Expensive)* comprises of a charming manor house and a number of cottages. The owner is millionaire Paul Lister, whose long-term goal is to turn the Scottish nature reserve into the kind of game reserves similar to those in South Africa.

To find out more about this wilderness area, visit the INSIDERTIP Croick Church nearby. Etched into its window panes are the farewells of the subsistence farmers who were driven off the land in May 1845. *www.alladale.com | 70 km/43.5 mi north of Inverness*

CAWDOR CASTLE ★ (134 B6) (*∅ J7*)

Its tower has stood here since 1372 and more than 200 years later, in 1606, William Shakespeare set his play 'Macbeth' in Cawdor Castle. In the play Macbeth belongs to the Campbell clan – and they are real – the Campbells of Cawdor have been living in the castle for 600 years but leave in the summer when paying visitors arrive to get a glimpse of what lies behind the castle's walls. There are a number of unique gardens, some are French inspired. *May–beginning Oct 10am–5pm | £12 | www.cawdorcastle.com | 22 km/13.7 mi north-east of Inverness*

CULLODEN BATTLEFIELD (134 A6) (*∅ J7*)

In 1746 Britain's last great battle took place here. Bonnie Prince Charlie had some men on his side but was defeated on the Highlanders moor by the Duke of Cumberland. The *Visitor Centre (daily Feb, March, Nov/Dec 10am–4pm, April–Oct 9am–5.30pm | £11)* details the battle. *7 km/4.4 mi east of Inverness*

DUNCANSBY HEAD (135 D1) (*∅ L3*)

Pure drama at Scotland's extreme northeastern point! After the leisurely views of the county of Caithness between Wick,

Probably one of Scotland's most beautiful views from Duncansby Head

Thurso, Scrabster (car ferrry to Orkney) and John o'Groats – attractive lodges are situated near the hotel with turrets that was refurbished to the north. Natural Retreats *(37 | rooms | tel. 01625 83 93 55 | short.travel/scot17 | Moderate–Expensive)* – offer breathtaking views 6 km/3.7 mi along the rocky coastline of the headland. The cliff faces are 80 m/262.5 ft high, while the Duncansby Stacks are 50 m/164 ft high and surrounded by more than a dozen different screaming seabirds. From mid-April to mid-July these are nesting grounds for common guillemots, razorbill auks, arctic skuas and fulmars. 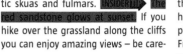 INSIDER TIP The red sandstone glows at sunset. If you hike over the grassland along the cliffs you can enjoy amazing views – be careful, as the wind often blows out to sea here. *194 km/121 mi north of Inverness*

DUNROBIN CASTLE AND GARDENS
(134 B4) *(⊞ J5)*

The stately home looks handsome, like a fairy-tale castle. The Earls of Sutherland have resided here for about 700 years. They were Britain's largest land owners, and after they concluded the highland clearances – the expulsion of local crofters – they were also the loneliest. Today, many tourists flock here and visit the glittering castle. The gardens are even better – like Versailles in the Highlands. The owners previously had 30 gardeners and were said to employ 100 staff for a party of 20 guests. From June to September daily falconry shows *(11.30am and 2pm, Sept Sun only 2pm)*. *April/May, Sept–mid-Oct daily 10.30am–4.30pm, June–Aug 10am–5pm | admission incl. castle, garden, falconry £11 | Dunrobin | 85 km/52.8 mi north of Inverness*

FINDHORN COMMUNITY ⊙
(134 B5) *(⊞ K6)*

Findhorn is a small experimental eco-community in the north-east of Scotland. The 400 or so residents of the remote village live in harmony with nature, produce food, have their own currency (Eko) and lead a simple life. 'Stop worrying' is what the road signs say. What started off in one caravan as a new age idea has since evolved into a spiritual community. There is a visitors' centre for day visitors and you can take a guided tour *(Jan, Dec 10am–12.15pm, Feb–Nov Mon–Fri 10am–5pm, May–Sept also Sat/Sun 1pm–4pm | guided tours £8)*. For guests spending the night there is a nice B & B (*Budget*) but they are welcome to become part of the community for a period of time. Findhorn's residents pass

on their knowledge through workshops and talks from self-awareness to personal environmental protection. *Findhorn near Forres | tel. 01309 69 03 11 | www.findhorn.org | 50 km/31.1 mi north-east of Inverness*

GLEN AFFRIC ☆ (129 E1) (*∅ H7*)

This has to be one of the most scenic Highland valleys in Scotland and home to the last forest of ancient Caledonian pine. Glen Affric is what the Highlands looked like before deforestation. Many hiking trails begin from *Loch Affric* (parking available at the privately-run Affric Lodge) among them a circular hiking trail around the loch (15 km/9.3 mi). A must for hikers is *Dog Falls*, a dramatic waterfall in a gorge below the dam. *45 km/28 mi south-west of Inverness*

LOW BUDGET

Dining in the Wild West: the remote ☆ *Applecross Inn (7 beds | Applecross | tel. 01520 74 42 62)* is well worth a detour just for the wonderful view of Raasay Island as well as its delicious, hearty and inexpensive meals.

Chlachaig Inn is the meeting place for international climbers. Sit around the fire and enjoy an inexpensive beer, generous portions of pub food and affordable good accommodation. *Daily | 5 km/3.1 mi from Glencoe village | tel. 01855 81 12 52*

Drover's Inn is a favourite among hikers on the West Highland Way. The bar serves excellent pies and succulent lamb. Camping *(£7)* on the farm next door.

LOCH NESS ★ (129 F1) (*∅ J7*)

It goes without saying that this lake south-west of Inverness has to be Scotland's most beautiful. It is 36 km/22.4 mi long and 1.5 km/0.9 mi wide and unusually deep at 325 m/1066 ft. The Loch Ness monster is still suspected to be lurking in its depths and the favourite lookout point for researchers is ● *Urquhart Castle* on the north-western shore near *Drumnadrochit* – a picturesque 12th century ruin. Drumnadrochit is also the centre of the 'Nessie' cult and has the best exhibition: *Loch Ness Exhibition Centre (Easter–June, Sept/Oct 9.30am–5pm, July/Aug 9.30am–6pm, Nov–Easter 10am–3.30pm | £7.95 | www.lochness.com).*

NORTH COAST ROAD TRIP
(133–134 D1–C6) (*∅ F3–L6*)

Scotland's most spectacular drive begins in Inverness and follows the northern coastal route for 830 km/516 mi. You can stay updated with the website and App (see p. 115). *www.northcoast500.com*

STIRLING

(130 B6) (*∅ J12*) **Stirling (pop. 45,000) was the capital of the Scottish kings in the Middle Ages and heavily fought over. The city is located strategically between the Low- and Highlands. The Wallace Monument is situated on the hill Abbey Craig.**

The historic old town is at the feet of the mighty Stirling Castle, not far from the Wallace Monument. Here, you are standing at the ex-front of the English and Scottish wars. Perhaps this is why the place is said to be haunted more than anywhere else in Scotland. The advantageous position on the Forth River and a slightly less harsh climate than in the north give Stirling a mild atmosphere.

SIGHTSEEING

LOCH LOMOND ★ (130 A6) (*H12*)

Scotland's largest and most popular lake. Geologically the Highlands begin on its southern shore; streets and a railway line run along its western shore; while the ● *West Highland Way* hiking trail is on its eastern shore. The most superb scenery is on the section that includes Rob Roy's cave hideaway (signposted) between Rowardennan, Inversnaid and the tiny INSIDERTIP Ardlui ferry departure point – where a mooring buoy has to be hoisted for a ride. The ferry means you shorten the hike to the pub, the *Drover's Inn* at Inverarnan (*£3*).

NATIONAL WALLACE MONUMENT ✂ (130 B5) (*J12*)

The Hollywood film 'Braveheart' introduced the whole world to the story of William Wallace. It was at Stirling Bridge, 2 km/1.2 mi south of Stirling, that the Scottish hero fought his famous battle in 1297. The museum houses his sword and if you brave the 246 stair climb to the top of the 67 m/219.8 ft high tower you will be rewarded with the most spectacular view towards the battlefield at Bannockburn. *Jan–March, Nov/Dec 10.30am–4pm, April–June, Sept/Oct 10am–4pm, July/Aug 10am–6pm | £9.99*

STIRLING CASTLE (130 B5) (*J12*)

A star attraction for all fans of myths and legends! Stirling Castle, like Edinburgh Castle perched high on a rock, was heavily fought over between about 1300 and 1700. The heroes William Wallace (1297, Stirling Bridge) and King Robert Bruce (1314) both captured the castle from the superior English. Mary Stuart was crowned Queen of Scots at the formidable castle in 1534 when she was barely a year old. There is an exhibition of the

Nessie lookout point: Urquhart Castle ruins

standard-bearers of the old Highland aristocracy. *April–Sept 9.30am–6pm, Oct–March 9.30am–5pm | £15*

FOOD & DRINK

HERMANN'S

An Austrian chef uses the best Scottish ingredients for his classic strudels, schnitzel and salmon – delicious! *Daily | Mar Place House | tel. 01786 45 06 32 | Moderate*

WHERE TO STAY

BREADALBANE HOUSE

At the southern end of the enchanting Loch Tay is the B&B owned by Dutch hosts. A modern guesthouse, despite the typical Highland facade. Enjoy the hospitality 60 km/37.3 mi north of Stirling on the way to Fort William. *5 rooms | Killin | tel. 01567 82 0134 | www.breadalbane house.com | Budget*

GLENEAGLES

This world-famous luxury hotel, which is located 30 km/18.6 mi north-east of Stirling, is set in acres of expansive parklands and includes the most renowned golf course. The championship greens were designed by leading British golf course architects and also the ● spa area is exceptional. Guests can enjoy special Balinese and Indian therapies; the one to try is the INSIDERTIP synchronised four-handed Purva Kar ma massage – pricey at £267 but well worth it. *222 rooms | Auchterarder | tel. 01764 66 22 31 | tel. in UK (freephone) 0800 3 89 37 37 | www.gleneagles.com | Expensive*

INFORMATION

STIRLING ICENTRE
Old Town Jail | St John Street | Stirling | tel. 01786 47 50 19 | www.visitscottish heartlands.com

WHERE TO GO

BLAIR CASTLE
(130 B3) (*∅ K10*)
This castle's whimsical fairytale appearance dates back to 1869 when the seventh Duke of Atholl, who had a weakness for Baronial architecture, had the then 600-year-old building refurbished. Today, valuable works of art, paintings and antiquities are exhibited in its 32 rooms. *April–Oct 9.30am–5.30pm | £11 | www.blair-castle.co.uk | 100 km/62 mi north of Stirling*

DUNDEE (131 D4) (*∅ L11*)
Scotland's fourth largest city (pop. 150,000) is situated in a fantastic location on the Tay estuary. It was famous for its jute industry and as the city where Robert F. Scott's expedition ship the Discovery *(Mon–Sat 10am–6pm, Sun 11am– 6pm | £9 | Discovery Quay)* was built. Nowadays, biomedicine, the digital entertainment industry, technical design and two universities are the main pillars. Over the next decade, the harbour front will be redeveloped to a high standard: in 2018, the outstanding foundation was the first Scottish design museum INSIDERTIP *Victoria & Albert Museum Dundee (www.vandadundee.org)*. It looks like a filigree, weathered ship's hull and was designed by the architect Kengo Kuma. In 2014, Dundee was Great Britain's first British Unesco City of Design. *85 km/52.8 mi north-east of Stirling*

FIFE ★ (131 D–E5) (*∅ L11–12*)
Between the estuaries of the Rivers Tay and Forth is the attractive peninsula of Fife, once known as the Kingdom of Fib under the Picts. It is worthwhile making a detour to the east on the journey from Edinburgh to Aberdeen, as soon as you have crossed the Forth Bridge. Along the coast, you will find the charming coastal towns of Pittenweem and Crail – you can still see their previous importance and wealth as fishing and trading ports. The town of Crail has expanded over the centuries with its many listed buildings and its architectural merits – like the red, steep roof-tops of Crail dating back to trade with the Dutch – it is pleasant to stroll through the streets and narrow alleys. Travelling further north you arrive at the world-famous city of golf. In St Andrews, where Prince William studied at Scotland's oldest university, you can see the greens of the most exclu-

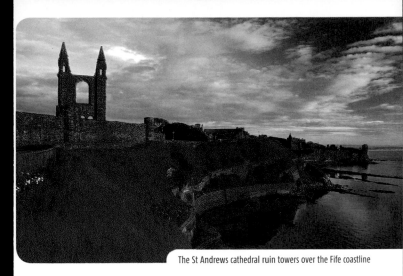

The St Andrews cathedral ruin towers over the Fife coastline

sive golf club and learn plenty of interesting facts about the game in the modern *British Golf Museum (April–Sept Mon–Sat 9.30am–5pm, Sun from 10am, Oct–March daily 10am–4pm | £8)*: Scotland regards itself as the guardian of the game. Further north, east of Tayport, the fabulous miles of beaches, sand dunes and forest invite you to go walking at INSIDER TIP *Tentsmuir* – watch out for seals at the headland. Treat yourself to a three-course reasonably priced lunch at the *The Peat Inn (8 rooms | Cupar | tel. 01334 84 02 06 | www.thepeatinn. co.uk | Budget–Moderate)*, one of Scotland's finest small country restaurants. *60 km/37.3 mi east of Stirling*

PERTH (130 C5) (*Ø K11*)

Perth was the capital of Scotland until 1452 and favoured, thanks to its ideal location on the River Tay, as a centre for wool and salmon. Today Perth (pop. 48,000) makes for an excellent springboard from which to set out for the Fife peninsula in the south-east, Stirling in the south-west or the Highlands in the north. *63 Tay Street (closed Mon | tel. 01738 44 14 51 | Moderate)* serves sumptuous Scottish-European cuisine at the address of the same name.

On the outskirts is *Scone Palace (April, Oct daily 10am–4pm, May–Sept 9.30am–5pm, Nov/Dec, Feb/March garden only (admission free) Fri–Sun 10am–4pm | £11.50 | www.scone-palace.co.uk)*. The palace was first built in 1808 – it houses ivory treasures and tapestries – and is situated close to a place of historic significance. A sign indicates the 152-kg/335-lbs sandstone rock on which Scottish kings were enthroned, known as the *Stone of Scone*. In 1296, King Edward I removed the stone to London as the spoils of war. It was last used in 1953 during the coronation of Queen Elizabeth – in its place under the coronation throne in Westminster Abbey. In 1996, the stone was then transferred to Edinburgh Castle, although it's uncertain whether this is still the original. *50 km/31.1 mi north-east of Stirling*

SCOTLAND AND ITS WHISKY

How do you explain that this distilled blend of barley is famous around the world? It's down to the Irish monks who imported the whiskey recipe to Scotland in the 14th century. Over time, the 'water of life' became known as 'whisky' – in Gaelic it's called *Uisge Beatha*. After centuries of illicit distilling, today the single malt is intelligently marketed as a luxury brand – Scotland's elixir of life in a bottle.

Whisky is produced in a single distillery from a mash barley, water and yeast. First the barley germinates, and then the germination process is halted by a heating process. The fire used in the drying process is often fed with sods of peat which gives many malt whiskies their distinctive, smoky taste. Then the the grain is crushed and mixed with locally sourced water. It separates into a sweet broth and grain waste – farmers generally use the waste as cattle feed – then yeast is added to ensure fermentation, and an alcoholic mash is created. This preliminary stage whisky is then distilled in copper kettles in a complex burning process. In this process, the middle distillate is mainly used because the pre and post flow are unpalatable.

The whisky gets its golden colour from storage in old sherry or bourbon barrels (plus the caramel colouring). The whisky must remain sealed in the barrels for three years under HM Customs and Excise supervision in order for it to be called as such. In the following years it will draw aromas from the wood. Scotland's more than 800 whiskies get their unique flavours from a combination of the shape of the individual stills, the wood which is used for the barrels, water from moor or heather and even the environment.

During the storage process some of the whisky will evaporate, and this percentage is known as the 'the angels' share' but the barrels also absorb the salty flavours of sea air.

FROM MALTS TO BLENDS

Scottish whisky is divided into three major groups. Firstly there is *grain whisky*, which is predominantly used as a mix, while *blended whisky* is blended to a uniform (brand) taste without any unwarranted surprises, and then there is *malt whisky* and malts are responsible for Scotland's reputation as a whisky nation. While single malts came from

From the peat flavour, angels' share and barley, fermenting and tasting: Everything you need to know about Scotland's elixir of life

a single distillery, the traditional Scotch malts are usually mixed blends. At the bottling stage water is added to the whisky to dilute it. Scotch has 40 per cent alcohol, other whiskies up to 46 per cent. Then there is the upper premium category of 'cask strength' whisky which is an acquired taste. This contains well over 50 per cent alcohol and tastes more intensive.

DISTINCTIVE DISTILLERIES

There are more than 100 active distilleries in Scotland. If you're after that distinctive smoky taste you have to head to Islay with its eight distilleries *(www. islaywhiskysociety.com)* or in the east Highlands you can drive along the ★ ● *Malt Whisky Trail (www.maltwhisky trail.com)*. This trail – actually, it includes several trails – is a feast for the tastebuds. The taste is more full-bodied than in the west – more banana, pear, chewing gum and no smoky taste.

The tours on Islay and Orkney (at the Highland Park), as well as Arran – which has only had an operational distillery since 1995 – are particularly well presented. The youngest distillery – INSIDER TIP *Wolfburn* near Thurso – produced its first three-year-old malt in 2016; it's delicious and almost without any smoky taste.

TIPS & TRICKS

Some Scotish restaurants also jump on the whisky bandwagon by offering dinners where a different malt whisky is served with every course. A feat to get through even for a whisky-resilient Scotsman!

So, how should whisky be taken? Neat or with a dash of water? It has been proven that a malt whisky releases the most aromas when served at room temperature with a dash of soft water added to it. However, some people swear by a good mix with Ginger Beer.

THE WEST COAST & HEBRIDES

Hav bred ey **(the islands at the edge of the sea) was the term the Vikings once used for the Hebrides. The Inner Hebrides are clearly visible from the mainland.**

While the Outer Hebrides lie far out in the Atlantic: a barren yet austerely beautiful paradise where tweed is woven and seals frolic in the bays and coves. Skye, the largest of the islands, is like a miniature version of Scotland's landscapes.

Small towns like Oban and Ullapool are ideal points from where to set out with your car, for a day trip with the ferry or a ride along the lonely western coastline. Those who decide to visit the west coast and the islands are bound to fall in love with them – and come back again.

OUTER HEBRIDES

(132 A–C 1–4, 133 D–*F1*–6) *(ٯٯ C–F 4–8)*

The Islands of Lewis, Harris, North and South Uist and Barra have fabulous sunsets. The romantic atmosphere, Gaelic feel and first-class accommodation have contributed to a small tourist boom.

Don't be surprised that Lewis and the rocky Harris are actually one and the same island. Its endless sandy beaches and magical stone circle helps you forget the urban atmosphere in Stornoway (pop. 8,000). North and South Uist are covered by Machair, the colourful wildflower meadows behind the beach.

Highlands and islands: anyone who has once visited the wild, romantic west coast and its islands will return time and again

SIGHTSEEING

BARRA
(137 D5–6) (*m C–D8*)

The island has long sandy beaches, an imposing castle, Gaelic culture and prehistoric ruins. *Castlebay* is its main town, and *Kisimul Castle* of the MacNeil clan stands firm on its island location. Ferries leave from and to Mallaig and Oban. A unique phenomenon is Barra's tide-dependent flight connection to Glasgow *(www.flybe.com)*: At low tide the INSIDER TIP beach is used as a runway and in stormy conditions the island is completely cut off from Barra.

CALLANISH STANDING STONES ★ ●
(124 A2) (*m E4*)

This 5000 year old place of worship on Lewis consists of 50 standing stones laid out in the shape of a cross around what may once have been a tomb. Its full magic unfolds at INSIDER TIP sunrise when, with a little luck, you could have the site all to yourself.

People could not settle on St Kilda. But visitors still return

GOLDEN ROAD ★ 🌿
(132 A4) (𝄞 E6)

A gem just like on Mars: here, Stanley Kubrick shot the scenes for his visionary science-fiction film '2001'. This single track tarmac road winds through the evocative, rocky landscape of East Harris dotted with tweed weavers cottages and isolated bays. The road gets its ironic name from the enormous cost of building it. Take the detour through the moors between Finsbay (for its seals) and Leverburgh (the ferry). Drop in at the lovely *Skoon Art Café (Tue–Sat 10am–4.30pm | Budget)* in *Geocrab* for cakes or a hearty bowl of soup in between paintings.

INSIDER TIP ST KILDA (0) (𝄞 B 5–6)

Did people live here? This question always comes up, because the archipelago lies some 80 km/50 mi west of Harris and is a remote collection of rock outcrops in the vast expanse of the Atlantic Ocean. Ever since the Neolithic era, people have tried to settle on St Kilda, but no civilisation has managed to live here permanently. In 1930 the last 36 islanders moved to the mainland leaving behind the wind, the feral sheep and legions of seabirds. Today the entire group of islands around the main island of Hirta is the property of the National Trust of Scotland, a Unesco World Heritage Site and one of Europe's most important bird sanctuaries. A trip to these Scottish outposts is unforgettable: basking sharks and whales cavort in the Atlantic, and puffins and Soay sheep cling to the steep cliffs above the coastlines. Abandoned houses and crumbling church ruins bear testimony to attempts to make the rough land habitable. A day trip (three hours travelling time each way and a six-hour walking tour on land) is very manageable from Leverburgh on South Harris. Motorboats do the trip out there. *From £225 | www. kildacruises.co.uk*

UIST ISLANDS (137 E3–5) (𝄞 D 6–8)

The islands of *North Uist*, *Benbecula* and *South Uist* are joined to one another by causeways. Motorists set out on ferries for Uist from Leverburgh on Harris or from Skye on Scotland's west coast. Benbecula has an airport. The islands are ideal for birdwatching and the *Balranald Nature Reserve* on North Uist is a bird sanctuary with 183 species among them oystercatchers and plovers. In the east of the island, the village of *Lochmaddy* offers kayaking, diving and rock climbing *(tel. 01876 50 04 80 | www.uistoutdoor centre.co.uk)*.

The western coast of South Uist has a 40 km/24.9 mi long beach covered in shells, set against a backdrop of dunes and wild flower meadows with bumble-bees *(machair)*. The eastern coast is rugged and interspersed with lakes.

FOOD & DRINK

SCARISTA HOUSE
(132 A4) (*ω D6*)

This very homely restaurant is first rate when it comes to the preparation of local products such as lamb and langoustines. Scarista House is part of a ☆ country house hotel *(6 rooms | Moderate)* wlth beautiful beach and mountain panorama. *Closed Jan and Feb | tel. 01859 55 02 38 | www.scaristahouse. com | Moderate*

BEACHES

SCARISTA BEACH
(132 A4) (*ω D6*)

This golden, fine sandy beach in western Harris is so beautiful and so romantic that some couples have tied the knot on it. To get there take the main road from Tarbert in the direction of Rodel. You'll see the beach after 15 km/9.3 mi. There are no kiosks for snacks so it is best to take a picnic basket, two glasses and a bottle of your favourite tipple and watch the sun go down.

WHERE TO STAY

INSIDER TIP BLUE REEF COTTAGES
● ◑ (132 A4) (*ω D6*)

Two unique, turf roofed stone cottages in the breathtaking coastal beauty of

Harris. You can enjoy the stunning panoramic views from the huge picture windows – the tides, the eagles, the clouds drifting by and the magnificent sunsets. The hosts run their establishment with the kind of sustainable luxury that is also evident in the thousands of trees they have planted to offset the carbon footprint. You'll find a welcome bottle of champagne and fair trade goods in the luxury kitchen. *Scarista | Harris | tel. 01859 55 03 70 | www.stay-hebrides. com | Expensive*

GEARRANNAN BLACKHOUSE VILLAGE
(132 A2) (*ω E4*)

The rustle of the thatch and smoke rising from the chimney of these restored cottages gives you a real feel for what it must have been like to live in a blackhouse crofting village. You will experience history when you spend the night in Carloway where an old seaside village has been restored and turned into

MARCO POLO HIGHLIGHTS

★ **Callanish Standing Stones**
A mystery to this day: Great Britain's largest ring of giant standing stones → p. 77

★ **Golden Road**
Take a drive on one of the world's most scenic roads → p. 78

★ **Trotternish Peninsula**
The Isle of Skye with its awe-inspiring coastline and massive mystical rock → p. 81

★ **Staffa**
Uninhabited and bizarre: the island off Mull is a natural wonder → p. 83

self-catering accommodation. *5 cottages | Carloway | Lewis | tel. 01851 64 34 16 | www.gearrannan.com | Moderate–Expensive*

HOTEL HEBRIDES (132 A4) *(∅ E5)*
Modern with a boutique hotel feel to it located in the North Harris ferry port. Both the bar and restaurant are surprisingly cool. Superb local cuisine! *21 rooms | Pier Road | Tarbert | Harris | tel. 01859 50 23 64 | www.hotel-hebrides.com | Moderate*

LOCHMADDY HOTEL (132 A5) *(∅ D6)*
An established hotel, with the cosy charm of a historical house, it is located near the ferry terminal, the *Centre for Gaelic Culture (taigh-chearsabhagh. org)* and an outdoor centre. Nice rooms, good meals and a range of single rooms. *15 rooms | Lochmaddy | North Uist | tel. 01876 50 03 31 | www.lochmaddyhotel. co.uk | Moderate*

SPORTS & ACTIVITIES

The main activity in this remote spot is to observe the landscape and the weather. In south Lewis, you can park your car on the B 887, 13 km/8.1 mi west of Tarbert, and climb to the summit of the dramatic and solitary INSIDER TIP *Glen Meavaig* to watch golden eagles from a hide.

INFORMATION

STORNOWAY ICENTRE
(132 B2) *(∅ F4)*
26 Cromwell Street | Stornoway | Lewis | tel. 01851 70 30 88 | www.visithebrides.com

FERRIES

Operator for the ferry service from the mainland to the islands is *Caledonian* *MacBrayne (tel. 0800 0 66 50 00 | www. calmac.co.uk).* For island hopping it is best to get the *Hebridean Hopscotch* ticket.

INNER HEBRIDES/SKYE

(132 A–C 5–6) *(∅ E–F 6–8)* **The Isle of Skye's name (Inner Hebrides) means 'clouds and mist'; its population is 10,000. But this isn't the whole truth – the island with the bridge encompasses the magic of Scotland.**
The diverse beauty of the island includes the dramatic *Cuillin* massif which is often covered in clouds. *Portree* is the picturesque main town in the east. Now that Skye is connected to the mainland by bridge, it is the only area of the Highlands and Islands that has recorded a rise in population figures.

SIGHTSEEING

CUILLINS
(128 B–C1) *(∅ F7–8)*
Sligachan, in the middle of the island, serves as a departure point for tours to the *Red Cuillin*. These are more easily accessible than the *Black Cuillin,* where the highest mountain, *Sgurr Alasdair*, is 993 m/3258 ft high. Those who prefer not to climb so high can head for the INSIDER TIP *Fairy Pools* to go swimming. A rugged path from Sligachan to Glenbrittle is 8 km/5 mi long; on the road from Carbost to Glenbrittle after 8 km/5 mi there is a car park which is close to the magical, secret spot to swim.

TALISKER DISTILLERY
(132 B6) *(∅ E7)*
The exquisite single malt from the west coast on the Isle of Skye has a histor-

ic reputation – Robert L. Stevenson already described it as the 'king o' drinks'. Talisker Distillery offers a guided tour with tasting – it's highly recommended. *July/Aug Mon–Fri 9.30am–5.30pm, Sat 9.30am–5pm, Sun 11am–5pm, always check for changes to the opening times | tour 45 min, £10 | Carbost | www.discovering-distilleries.com/talisker*

TROTTERNISH PENINSULA ★
(132 B–C5) (*ᗰ F6*)

The *Old Man of Storr* looks like a menhir and towers 48 m/157.5 ft above a picture-perfect coastline. At Staffin you can see how the rock was torn apart some 50 million years ago causing columns of 'pleats' in the aptly named *Kilt Rock*. At the northern end of the peninsula are the jagged *Quiraing* rock formations The standing stone is the backdrop in the "Alien" prequel "Prometheus".

THE GLENVIEW
(132 C5) (*ᗰ F6*)

Anyone who loves the peace and quiet on the island and wants to arrive early after the hike at Quiraing will find the perfect hotel location here, and dinner. *5 rooms | 6.5 km/4 mi south of Staffin on the A 855 | tel. 01470 56 22 48 | www.glenviewskye.co.uk | Moderate*

THREE CHIMNEYS RESTAURANT
(132 B6) (*ᗰ E7*)

An award-winning restaurant in an old crofter's cottage, serving exquisite cuisine. Exclusive accommodation offered in six rooms if you want to stay on longer. *Daily | Colbost, Dunvegan | tel. 01470 51 12 58 | www.threechimneys.co.uk | Expensive*

PORTEE ICENTRE (132 C5) (*ᗰ F7*)
Bayfield House | Portree | tel. 01478 61 29 92 | www.skye.co.uk

PLOCKTON (133 D6) (*ᗰ G7*)
This picturesque town is straight out of a story book! Its mild climate is influenced by the warm Gulf Stream which is why the palm-like cabbage trees thrive here. Old fishing and farming cottages huddle around the bay – today they serve as shops and hotels. Spend the night and enjoy a meal at the *Plockton Hotel*

Bizarre rock on Skye: the 'Old Man of Storr'

(14 rooms | 41 Harbour Street | tel. 01599 54 42 74 | www.plocktonhotel.co.uk | Moderate). 12 km/7.5 mi east of Skye

RAASAY (132 C5–6) (*Ø F6–7*)
The remote hostel and hotel *Raasay House (13 rooms | tel. 01478 66 02 66 | www.raasay-house.co.uk | Budget–Moderate)* on Raasay Island is a beautifully renovated former country house. It's a great base for climbing, sailing, kayaking at the outdoor centre. *Ferry from Sconser (Skye)*

SMALL ISLES
(128 B–C 2–3) (*Ø E–F 9–10*)
Muck, *Eigg* and *Rùm* are ideal destinations for island hopping. From the captivating fishing port of *Mallaig* you can take the 'Shearwater' *(www.arisaig.co.uk)*. The timetable offers a short stay before the boat returns. *Rùm* is a nature island (no residents) with *Kinloch Castle* which gives an insight into the lifestyle of rich industrialists about 100 years ago. About 80 people live on the volcanic rock of the island of *Eigg* – they joined forces to buy their island after they had had enough of playboys and artists as landlords. *www.road-to-the-isles.org.uk*
From Mallaig you can take the ferry (30 minutes) to Scotland's remotest and great pub, INSIDER TIP *The Old Forge (Budget–Moderate)* in Inverie on Loch Nevis. Serves pizza with seafood and game, and B&B.

OBAN

(129 D5) (*Ø G11*) **This sickle-shaped, small town (population 9000), is regarded as the gateway to the Hebrides, a bustling fishing port with hotels and restaurants.**
Its landmark is a replica of the Colosseum in Rome, called *MacCaig's Folly*, which John Stewart MacCaig had built in 1897.

SIGHTSEEING

OBAN DISTILLERY
A whisky with a hint of peat has been produced here since 1794. Tours available. *Closed Jan and Feb | £8 | Stafford Street | tel. 01631 57 20 04 | www.discovering-distilleries.com/oban*

FOOD & DRINK

EE-USK
In Gaelic *ee usk* means fish, just what this chic seafood and wine bar on the new harbour waterfront of Oban does best. A variety of fresh fish and shellfish and French wines. *Daily | North Pier | tel. 01631 56 56 66 | www.eeusk.com | Moderate*

WHERE TO STAY

GLENBURNIE HOUSE
Oban's most popular B&B has the atmosphere of a friendly coastal hotel. *12 rooms | Corran Esplanade | tel. 016 31 56 20 89 | www.glenburnie.co.uk | Moderate*

INFORMATION

OBAN ICENTRE
3 North Pier | Argyll | Oban | tel. 01631 56 31 22 | www.oban.org.uk

FERRIES

From Oban you can catch a ferry to the Inner and Outer Hebrides. *Ferry Terminal (tel. 01631 56 66 88 | www.calmac.co.uk)*

WHERE TO GO

INVERARAY (129 E5) (*Ø G11*)
A picturesque village (population 800) on *Loch Fyne* with a Georgian *castle (www.inveraray-castle.com)* and prison

museum *(www.inverarayjail.co.uk)* dating back to 1820. *65 km/40.4 mi south-east of Oban*

ISLAY & JURA
(124 A–B 1–2) (᠓ E–F 13–14)

Aside from eight distilleries *Islay* (pop. 3500) is also home to the first whisky academy *(www.islaywhiskysociety. com)* in Scotland. Here you can learn more about whisky nosing and etiquette as well as about the kinds of food that go best with whisky. A good accommodation option is the *Glenmachrie House (5 rooms | tel. 01496 302560 | www. glenmachrie.co.uk | Moderate)* north of Port Ellen.

The trip from Islay (Port Askaig) to *Jura* only takes a few minutes. The island is sparsely populated, with just 200 inhabitants, but does have some 5000 red deer. In 1946–47 George Orwell completed his oppressive novel, '1984' while on the island. *South-west of Oban*

MULL *(128 B–C 4–5) (᠓ E–F 10–11)*

A haven for mountain hikers, with sea eagles overhead and mature island cheese *(www.isleofmullcheese.co.uk)*. *Tobermory's* colourful houses represent Mull's party mile. The highlight is the free concerts of the famous music festival ● *Mendelssohn on Mull* in July. *West of Oban*

STAFFA ★ *(128 B4) (᠓ E11)*

Listen to the inspiration for the composer! Stream Felix Mendelssohn Bartholdy's "Hebrides Overture" through your earphones, while you take a boat trip to the basalt columns of the 80-m/262.5-ft long mini-island and *Fingal's Cave*. Boats to the island leave from Iona and Fionnphort on Mull *(daily | from £30 | www.staffatours.com | www.staffa trips.co.uk)*. You can only disembark in calm weather.

TIREE & COLL
(128 A–B 3–4) (᠓ D–E 10–11)

These two islands, between the Inner and Outer Hebrides, offer the most hours of sunshine and are idyllically secluded. They epitomise the true desert island setting – dunes and white sandy beaches. *Tiree* (pop. 760) is a windsurfer paradise

A marvel of nature: the basalt pillars of the Hebridean island of Staffa

A fairy-tale setting: Ullapool port bathed in blue – it's high time for a *pint*

and hosts an international surf festival in October while *Coll* (pop. 150) is scattered with Stone Age relics. Both islands have cosy hotels that offer full board and lodging and excellent seafood: *Scarinish Hotel (Tiree | tel. 01879 22 03 08 | Moderate)* or *Coll Hotel (tel. 01879 23 03 34 | Moderate). To get there: ferry (www.calmac.co.uk) or light aircraft (www.hebrideanair.co.uk) from Oban*

ULLAPOOL

(133 E4) (*⌘ G6*) Is this the end of the world? Ullapool (pop. 1500) feels a bit like this with its white cottages projecting into Loch Broom. It's the last stop before the North Highlands.

It is from here that the ferries depart to Lewis and Harris in the Outer Hebrides, and from here there are excursions to the *Summer Isles*, a group of small islands where you can watch seals, dolphins and birds *(tours operated by Shearwater Cruises | £35 per 3h |* *tel. 01854 61 24 72 | www.summer queen.co.uk).*

FOOD & DRINK/ WHERE TO STAY

THE CEILIDH PLACE ●
This establishment feels like a home away from home: cosy restaurant *(Moderate)*, a wonderful book store, charming hotel and inviting hostel all in one. *13 rooms | 14 West Argyle St | tel. 01854 61 21 03 | www.theceilidhplace.com | Budget–Moderate*

MACKAY'S ⭐ (129 F1) (*⌘ H4*)
In this remote spot on the beaches of the wild north-east coast is a traditional country hotel which has been tastefully refurbished. Serves excellent food. The 7 rooms are cosy and modern, the views are fabulous.
Durness | tel. 01971 51 12 02 | www.visit durness.com | Moderate | Luxury cottages £1500 (Sat–Sat) | 109 km/68 mi north of Ullapool

THE WEST COAST & HEBRIDES

INFORMATION

TOURIST OFFICE
6 Argyle Street | tel. 01854 612486 (*)

WHERE TO GO

CAPE WRATH (133 E1) (*∭ H3*)
Take either the ferry or the minibus from *Durness* to the cliffs and the lighthouse *(daily May–Sept)* or go on a hike along the challenging but breathtaking 28 km/17.4 mi coastline between the Cape and *Kinlochbervie. www.visit capewrath.com | 70 km/43.5 mi north of Ullapool*

HANDA ISLAND (133 E2) (*∭ G–H 4*)
The boat trip to the bird island takes 30 minutes from the remote Tarbet Pier north of Scourie. A 2.5 km/1.6 mi walk ends with a 350 m/1148 ft high cliff densely populated with seabirds and if you scramble over the rock along the coast, you'll get pretty close to the seals *(from £20 | www.scouriewildlifecruises. co.uk)*. Highly recommended: round off your trip with a visit to the castle in Tarbet and enjoy a seafood meal afterwards at the *Shorehouse Seafood Restaurant (April–Sept Mon–Sat, noon–8pm | tel. 01971 502251 | Budget)*.

INVEREWE GARDENS ●
(133 D4) (*∭ G6*)
In 1862 when Osgood Mackenzie put a fence around three plants, he had no idea that this would result in one of the most northerly botanical gardens in the world. Located right by the sea, the Inverewe Gardens are divided into themed sections and are a paradise of exotic and subtropical plants. *April–Oct 10am–5pm, Jan–March, Nov/Dec 10am–3pm | £10.50 | Poolewe | 80 km/49.7 mi south of Ullapool*

LOCHINVER
(133 E3) (*∭ G5*)
The coastal port feels like it is exposed to the Atlantic, and you reach it via the dramatic A 837. First, you pass the remote *Loch Assynt* with the romantic fortress ruin *Ardvrech Castle*. 2 km/1.2 mi south of here you can park and hike along the limestone trail to *Bone Cave* (4.5-km/2.8-mi round tour). Cyclists can ride for 60–70 km/37.3–43.5 mi on narrow routes – pre-book the cycles at *The Rose Guest House (tel. 01571 844257 | www.the-rose-bb.com)*. The local *Assynt Foundation (www.assyntfoundation.org)* has purchased a typical stretch of the Highlands from the owners and is modernising the region. The centrepiece is the large hunting villa Glencanisp Lodge *(26 rooms | tel. 01571 844100 | www.glencanisp-lodge.co.uk | Moderate–Expensive)*, where you should enquire about last-minute offers.

LOW BUDGET

The *Gatliff Trust Hotels* in Rhenigidale, Berneray and Howmore are three rustic and inexpensive accommodation options in the Outer Hebrides for backpackers. Locals now run the old traditional crofthouses, once inhabited by farmers, as hostels. Peat fires and showers.

The *Caledonian MacBrayne* shipping company *(tel. 0800 0 66 50 00 | www.calmac.co.uk)* offers an Island Rover ticket that permits you to visit as many islands as you like in 8 *(£57)* or 15 *(£82)* days. Motor cars from £267, bicycles free of charge.

ORKNEY & SHETLAND

The Pentland Firth is a strait that separates the melancholy of the Highlands from the wide open pastures and beautiful, sandy beaches of Orkney.

Some 21,000 Orcadians engage in livestock farming on 20 of the 86 islands and their relative wealth stems from the fact that during World War I they sold produce to the English based in the *Scapa Flow* inland sea. The farmers used the money earned to purchase their own farmland, releasing them from the land barons.

Orkney's inhabitants are first and foremost farmers while the opposite is true for the 23,000 Shetlanders, most of whom are in the fishing industry. Some of them rear also a few sheeps and Shetland ponies.

Orkney, whose settlement goes back some 5000 years, is testimony to how its inhabitants made this remote northern region work for them. Shetland continues to draw visitors with its rustic charm, great diversity of bird life and the magical light display of the aurora borealis.

ORKNEY ISLANDS/ MAINLAND

(135 D–F 1–3) (*m K–M 1–3*) **The main islands of the Orkney Islands are influenced by farming. People have settled here for centuries.**

Welcome to Orcadia: on the trail of seabirds, the Northern Lights and the Atlantic island way of life

Stretching out to 35 km/21.8 mi by 20 km/12.4 mi is *Mainland (Orkney)* the largest of the islands in the archipelago. There are beaches right around the island and some magnificent cliffs on its western coast. On an isthmus between east and west Mainland is *Kirkwall* (pop. 9000), the bustling main town with its harbour pier and beautiful sandstone cathedral. The small airport is only a few miles from Kirkwall, and the ferry from Thurso takes about two hours.

SIGHTSEEING

ITALIAN CHAPEL ● ☀
(135 E3) (*ΩΩ L3*)

In 1943 Italian prisoners of war were deployed in Kirkwall to build concrete barriers between the islands to deter German submarines, while on the island they converted two Nissen huts into an a small but impressive chapel. The altarpiece depiction of the Madonna and Child was done using a Christmas card as a template. A touching building with

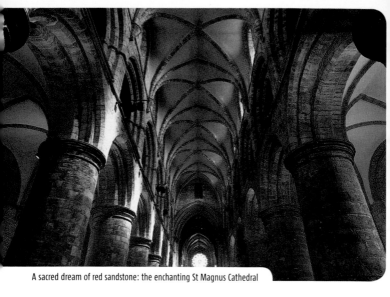

A sacred dream of red sandstone: the enchanting St Magnus Cathedral

lovely sea views. *7 km/4.4 mi south of Kirkwall*

MAES HOWE ● (135 E2) *(ⅅ L2)*

You have to crouch to get through the low passage to enter into this 5000 year old chamber tomb at Finstown. In the 12th century the Vikings probably used it to shelter from storms. They left behind some carved runic graffiti on the walls, the characters sing the praises of a certain 'beautiful Ingeborg', and today the inscriptions are used on jewellery made in Orkney. The magnificent tomb forms part of the so-called *Heart of Neolithic Orkney* Unesco World Heritage Site together with the Ring of Brodgar, Skara Brae and the Standing Stones of Stenness. *10 km/6.2 mi west of Kirkwall*

ORKNEY MUSEUM (135 E2) *(ⅅ L2)*

A must-see: in Tankerness House, opposite Kirkwall's cathedral, the museum documents the amazing 5000 year old history of Orkney. *Mon–Sat 10.30am–5pm | Broad Street*

INSIDER TIP PIER ARTS CENTRE (135 E3) *(ⅅ L2)*

A great gallery for high-quality art, located on a pier in Stromness harbour. *Tue–Sat 10.30am–5pm | 28–36 Victoria Street | www.pierartscentre.com*

NESS OF BRODGAR ★ (135 E2) *(ⅅ L2)*

Orkney's archaeological stone finds are internationally renowned. New excavations are concentrated on the narrow strip of land known as Ness of Brodgar. Here, over an area of 1 km/0.6 mi the spectacular *Ring of Brodgar* still has 27 large stones up to 4.7 m/15.4 ft high (twice as many as the more recent Stonehenge), and south of here is the *Barnhouse Settlement* and the older *Standing Stones of Stenness*. In 2002, in the middle of the site a farmer who was ploughing his field discovered an ancient living and cult site. Since then, a 6-acre large wall was revealed with houses and temples, and open at the end. Elements of wall frescoes were also exposed. A visit to the Neolithic urban settlement is a must! It's possible that the occupants at some point set off for present-day south England due to the climate, and taking their building knowledge with them. *www.orkneyjar.com | 8 km/5 mi east of Stromness*

SKARA BRAE ★ (135 D2) (*Ø L2*)

This is the best preserved Neolithic settlement in Europe: the ruins of the village on the west coast provide fascinating evidence of how people lived here 5000 years ago. In 1850 a storm stripped off the earth and uncovered the cluster of eight homes. *April–Sept 9.30am–5.30pm, Oct–March 9.30am–4.30pm | £7.10 | 30 km/18.6 mi north-west of Kirkwall*

ST MAGNUS CATHEDRAL
(135 E2) (*Ø L2*)

In 1137, this magnificent pink sandstone cathedral was built right by the sea. Today, it is in the middle of Kirkwall and is still one of the most beautiful churches in northern Europe.

STROMNESS (135 E3) (*Ø L2*)

This former herring fishing harbour was where the North Sea expeditions took their drinking water on board. The small town (population 2000) has to be one of northern Scotland's most melancholy and poetic places. It has incredibly narrow alleys and you'll want to while away some time listing to live music in its pubs. Stromness is the perfect stepping stone to the enchanting Isle of Hoy (30min by ferry) and for diving excursions in the *Scapa Flow*. Next to the campsite at the harbour is a ❧ INSIDER TIP golf course with fabulous views.

YESNABY SEA STACKS &
MARWICK HEAD (135 D2) (*Ø L2*)

The dramatic cliffscapes of *Yesnaby Sea Stacks* and *Marwick Head* on the northwestern coast of Mainland attract hikers and birdwatchers from May to August to see the thousands of breeding seabirds (such as puffins, fulmars and skaus) up close.

FOOD & DRINK

JUDITH GLUE REAL FOOD CAFE AND
RESTAURANT (135 E2) (*Ø L2*)

You can kill two birds with one stone and buy Judith's typical Orkney knitwear. Then enjoy the taste of Orkney with cheese, ale, seafood and whisky. *Daily, seasonal changing opening hours | 25 Broad Street | tel. 01856 87 42 25 | www.judithglue.com/pages/real-food-cafe | Budget–Moderate*

MARCO POLO HIGHLIGHTS

★ **Ness of Brodgar**
Northern Europe's first 'towns-people' lived between two stone circles → p. 88

★ **Skara Brae**
This well preserved Neolithic settlement remained buried under sand dunes for centuries → p. 89

★ **Hoy**
Orkney's second-largest island boasts huge colonies of puffins and a bizarre red sandstone coast → p. 91

★ **Broch of Mousa**
Eerie and atmospheric in the evening: the Pictish round tower in a breathtaking setting → p. 92

JULIA'S CAFÉ (135 E3) (*ℳ L2*)
Pies, cakes and vegetarian food served from early till late, at Julia's everything is home-made. Popular with the locals. *Daily | 20 Ferry Road | Stromness | tel. 01856 85 09 04 | Budget*

SHOPPING

Mainland is a shopper's paradise for those after high-quality crafts that reflect the rich regional culture. The creations inspired by nature, or the Nordic and Celtic myths from its more than 5000 years of history, are not to be missed. The *Orkney Craft Trail (www.orkneydesignercrafts.com)* leads you to individual studio addresses.

HIGHLAND-PARK DISTILLERY (135 E2) (*ℳ L2*)
Whisky has been distilled here since 1798. The slightly smoky drink is highly regarded among connoisseurs. Tra-

dition is carefully conserved at Highland Park: here you can still watch INSIDERTIP **floor malting**. *April–Sept Mon–Sat 10am–5pm, May–Aug also Sun noon–5pm, Oct–March Mon–Fri 1pm–5pm | from £7.50 | Holm Road | Kirkwall | tel. 01856 87 46 19 | www.highlandpark.co.uk*

SPORTS & ACTIVITIES

INSIDERTIP **SCAPA FLOW DIVING**
Scapa Flow (135 E3) (*ℳ L2*) lies between the islands of Mainland, Hoy and South Ronaldsay and is almost like an inland sea. Right in the middle of it at a depth of between 26 m/85.3 ft and 46 m/151 ft are half a dozen sunken German warships from World War I. Excursions for experienced scuba divers start from Stromness. Information and equipment: *The Diving Cellar (4 Victoria Street | Stromness | tel. 01856 85 00 55 | www.divescapaflow.co.uk)*

The Old Man of Hoy – a dramatic landmark on the second-largest of the Orkney Islands

AYRE HOTEL (135 E2) *(Ⓜ L2)*
A dignified, country house atmosphere in the main town in Kirkwall: tea is served in the garden. *33 rooms | Ayre Road | Kirkwall | tel. 01856 87 30 01 | www.ayre hotel.co.uk | Moderate*

STROMNESS HOTEL
(135 E3) *(Ⓜ L2)*
Comfortable hotel in an historic building with cosy, traditional bar popular with locals. Ask for a room overlooking the working harbour. *42 rooms | The Pierhead | Stromness | tel. 01856 85 02 98 | www.stromnesshotel.com | Moderate*

KIRKWALL ICENTRE (135 E2) *(Ⓜ L2)*
West Castle Street | Kirkwall | tel. 01856 87 28 56 | www.visitorkney.com

HOY ★ (135 D–E3) *(Ⓜ K–L3)*
The only island with a genuine Highland feeling. After the short ferry trip from Stromness *(three to four times daily | tel. 01856 87 20 44)*, you hike across a valley to the dramatic Rackwick Bay in the west, where you can watch the skuas hunting for prey – or diving furiously around your head if they have youngsters. The connecting cliff path is also used by puffins. At the end of the hike is the solitary rock spire the Old Man of Hoy, which is the red landmark of the second largest Orkney island. *www.hoyorkney.com*

NORTH RONALDSAY
(135 F1) *(Ⓜ M1)*
Miles away! As if symbolic of the life of a small isolated island community, a 21 km/13.1 mi long stone dyke surrounds this remote Orkney Island. It keeps the sheep away from the pastures and forces them towards a diet of kelp and seaweed in an area that is home to plenty of seals and seabirds. Worth the two-and-a-half hour cruise from Kirkwall for its stunning sandy beach, the wind and solar energy powered ◎ *Bird Observatory (www. nrbo.co.uk)*, as well as the old stone lighthouse. Tip: spend the night on the island at the nature centre's *Observatory Hostel (10 beds | tel. 01857 63 32 00 | Budget)* and then fly back by light aircraft *(www. loganair.co.uk)* afterwards – an amazing sightseeing adventure. Info: *www.orkney ferries.co.uk*

PAPA WESTRAY ◎ (135 E1) *(Ⓜ L1)*
This small (it is only 3.5 mi²), fair trade island is in the northern part of the archipelago, where the North Sea meets the Atlantic. The fair-trade status was awarded because every one of the 70 islands upholds fair trade practices. The residents have organised themselves as a co-operative to maintain fair trade, to convert empty houses into accommodation, to open a nature reserve and protect listed monuments, including the Neolithic home, the *Knap of Howar*, a hogback or carved Viking gravestone dating back to the 12th century as well as the manor house *Holland Farm* (17th century).
If you need some excitement after the peace and quiet of the island, you can consider leaving by plane. The INSIDER TIP world's shortest scheduled flight operates between Papa Westray and the larger island of Westray: it takes just two minutes! Once on Westray you should not miss the pride of the island: a small 5000 year old sandstone Neolithic figurine, the 'Orkney Venus', which was discovered in 2009. A year later archaeologists discovered a second figurine at the same site. *www. westraypapawestray.co.uk*

SHETLAND ISLANDS/ MAINLAND

(136 A–C 1–5) (*B–C 1–3*) **The narrow and elongated Mainland, the largest of the Shetland Islands, is characterised by rugged bays and scenic fjords or voes.** *Lerwick* (pop. 7500) is the main town, most important harbour and heart of this windswept hilly island. The scenery here is like the Highlands in miniature with a number of beautiful, sandy beaches and a dramatic rocky coastline. To the south is the airport, the *Sumburgh Head* cliff, the wreck of the oil tanker 'Braer' and archaeological excavations. All the place names and geographical references reflect the Norse heritage from the Vikings who settled here in the 9th century. To this day Scotland's northernmost inhabitants still have a greater affinity for Norway than Edinburgh or London.

LOW BUDGET

Great accommodation in an excellent location: *Hamnavoe Hostel (13 beds | from £20 | tel. 01856 85 12 02 | 10a North End Road | Stromness)* is in a wonderfully atmospheric coastal village.

Self-catering *Shetland on a shoestring: Camping Böds (April–Sept | from £10 | www.camping-bods.co.uk)* are nine inexpensive and very basic cottages and are all in great locations with an interesting history. *Own sleeping bag and camping stove needed.*

SIGHTSEEING

BROCH OF MOUSA ★ (136 B4) (*B3*)
Brochs were the double-walled residential towers of the Picts and this one, standing 13 m/42.7 ft tall, is Scotland's mightiest. Located on the island of Mousa, it is shrouded in a eerie atmosphere at dusk when thousands of small, black storm petrels fly up from the rocky beach below it. *Admission free | ferry from Sandwick*

JARLSHOF (136 B5) (*B3*)
The showpiece of archaeological evidence of settlement in the North Atlantic, it takes you on a journey from the Stone and Bronze Ages, Picts and Viking eras, the Middle Ages to the modern era. *April–Sept 9.30am–5.30pm, Oct–March 9.30am–sunset | £5.50 | Sumburgh Head*

SCALLOWAY (136 B4) (*B3*)
Distinctive for its over 400 year old fortress ruin, silhouetted against the harbour backdrop, this was once the capital of the Shetland Islands – to view *Scalloway Castle* you have to collect the key from the Royal Hotel. *Scalloway Museum* details the role that the town played in World War II when Scalloway (pop. 1300) was the headquarters of the Norwegian resistance. This is where the so-called *Shetland Bus* boat escape route to and from the Nazi occupied Norway was based. From 1940 thousands of Norwegians were rescued via the sea route – initially with fishing boats then later with some fast submarine chasers.

ST NINIAN'S ISLE (136 B4) (*B3*)
At low tide a golden sandy beach extends all the way to this offshore island where the remains of a church and a Celtic silver treasure have been found.

FOOD & DRINK

BUSTA HOUSE HOTEL (136 B3) (*B3*)
A romantic country house hotel (*22 rooms | Expensive*) that combines history with hospitality. The finest cuisine on Shetland! *Daily | Brae | tel. 01806 52 25 06 | www.bustahouse.com | Moderate–Expensive*

SPIGGIE HOTEL (136 B4) (*B3*)
A quiet country hotel (*6 rooms | Moderate*) with lobster, lamb and fresh eggs (restaurant Thu–Sat evenings | *Moderate*) *Daily | Scousburgh | tel. 01950 46 04 09 | Moderate*

WHERE TO STAY

SUMBURGH HOTEL (136 B5) (*B3*)
A stay at this manor house is well worth it for the atmosphere and views, the excellent salmon and its proximity to the spectacular cape, *Sumburgh Head*. 32 rooms | Sumburgh | tel. 01950 46 02 01 | www.sumburghhotel.com | Moderate*

INFORMATION

LERWICK ICENTRE (136 B4) (*B3*)
Market Cross | Lerwick | tel. 01595 69 34 34 | www.shetland.org

ISLANDS IN THE AREA

FAIR ISLE
(136 A–B6) (*B4*)
Set apart between Orkney and Shetland is the island (pop. 55) with the famous knitwear pattern. Sheep, cliffs, sea- and migratory birds attract the visitors who stay in the Bird Observatory (*Budget*). *Ferry (Tue, Thu, Sat | £20 | tel. 01595 76 03 63) from Grutness, flights from and to Lerwick (Mon–Sat | £85 | www.airtask.com). www.fairisle.org.uk*

A family affair: sheep breeders on the Shetland Islands

INSIDER TIP **FOULA** (136 A4) (*A3*)
On the wild island with 370-m/1214-ft high cliffs and the Gaada Stack rock formation in the sea, in the summertime the nesting seabirds take control. They even attack the 38 islanders who are out peat cutting. Accommodation: Leraback Bed & Breakfast (*3 rooms | tel. 01595 75 32 26 | www.originart.eu/leraback/leraback.html | Budget | full pension from around £60*). A small ferry leaves from Walls or Scalloway (*Tue, Thu, Sat | £15 | tel. 01595 84 02 08*) about two hours to Foula, return ferry always on the next day. 15-minute flight from Tingwall (*Mon, Tue, Wed, Fri | £79 return flight | www.airtask.com*).

UNST ✵ (136 C1) (*C1*)
One of the Shetland's most northerly points is here on the island: *Herma Ness*. The headland is haven for hikers with superb views over the bird-covered coast all the way to the lighthouse! Easily accessible by car via the roll-on roll-off ferry.

DISCOVERY TOURS

❶ SCOTLAND AT A GLANCE

START: ❶ Edinburgh END: ❶ Edinburgh	**9 days** Actual driving time 45 hours
Distance: 🚗 2225 km/1383 mi	

COSTS: approx. £980/$1350 per person (accommodation, food, admissions)

WHAT TO PACK: binoculars

IMPORTANT TIPS: Book hotel accommodation in advance! The same applies for bicycle hire in ㉑ **Lochinver** and dinner at ㉚ **The Peat Inn**!

In Scotland the traffic is light. You will travel past some breathtaking countryside. From Edinburgh head in a clockwise direction through the Borders in the warm

Would you like to explore the places that are unique to this country? Then the Discovery Tours are just the thing for you – they include terrific tips for stops worth making, breathtaking places to visit, selected restaurants and fun activities. It's even easier with the Touring App: download the tour with map and route to your smartphone using the QR Code on pages 2/3 or from the website address in the footer below – and you'll never get lost again even when you're offline.

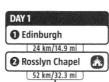

TOURING APP

→ p. 2/3

south, across the highlands of the west coast and making a detour to Skye. It is more isolated in the North Highlands, whereas more visitors head for the east in the forest and whisky regions along the River Spey.

From ❶ **Edinburgh** → p. 42 head on the A 8, A 720 and A 703 for the mythical place of ❷ **Rosslyn Chapel** → p. 51. On the trail of Scotland's myths, continue into Walter Scott's heartland of the Borders Region along the River Tweed. From the **A 6094 in Roslin**, head east to the

DAY 1

❶ Edinburgh

24 km/14.9 mi

❷ Rosslyn Chapel

52 km/32.3 mi

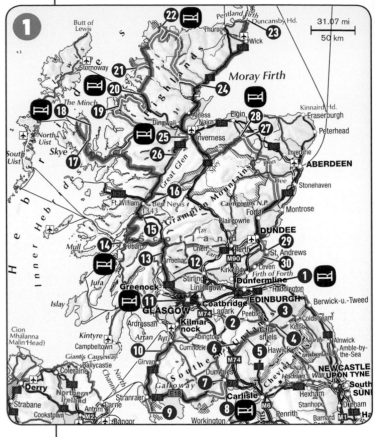

③ Abbotsford House 🏛
16 km/9.9 mi

④ Dryburgh Abbey 🏠
51 km/31.7 mi

⑤ Tibbie Shiels Inn 🍴
9 km/5.6 mi

⑥ Grey Mare's Tail 🥾 🌳
1 km/0.6 mi

⑦ Burns House 🏛
21 km/13.1 mi

⑧ Steamboat Inn 🍴 🛏
139 km/86 mi

A 7, and carry on southwards, where you will soon reach Scott's dream location of **③ Abbotsford House** → p. 34. Passing the ruins of Melrose Abbey you will find Scott's grave under the cedars in **④ Dryburgh Abbey** → p. 35. With so many cultural insights, carry on over the Highland route **A 708** → p. 34. Stop at the quaint **⑤ Tibbie Shiels Inn** → p. 35 at St Mary's Loch, where Scott also sought refreshment. A ten-minute drive further south and you can head on a hiking trail to the waterfall **⑥ INSIDER TIP Grey Mare's Tail**. **On the A 701 you reach Dumfries,** where at the **⑦ Burns House** you can learn more about the national poet → p. 38. Stay overnight in the **⑧ Steamboat Inn** → p. 38 further south on the coast.

DISCOVERY TOURS

Continuing on the south coast on the **A 75 to Stranraer, then south via the A 718 and A 716,** you arrive at the sub-tropical **⑨ Logan Botanic Gardens → p. 40**. There are fabulous views along the coast. The next highlight is a visit to the majestic **⑩ Culzean Castle → p. 39. Now leave the coast and head on the A 77 for the hip, post-industrial city of ⑪ Glasgow → p. 52**. Stay overnight in the central **Millennium Hotel → p. 57** at George Square and enjoy a typical Scottish dinner at **The Ubiquitous Chip → p. 55**. Next day, head westwards via the **M 8. Then, change to the east bank of the River Clyde and onto the A 82 in Kilpatrick.** You quickly arrive in **⑫ Loch Lomond → p. 71** and enjoy the view of the lake on the right-hand side. Relax in the cosy atmosphere of the traditional Highland pub **⑬ Drover's Inn → p. 70** in Inverarnan. **In Tyndrum, head in a westerly direction onto the M 85.** In **⑭ Oban → p. 82** stroll through the busy harbour towards the island ferries. You can find accommodation at **Glenburnie House → p. 82**.

Heading northwards on the **A 85 you reach the wonderful old Connel Bridge.** The next hour of the drive is also picturesque along the rocky coastline via the **A 828 into the magical valley of ⑮ Glen Coe → p. 66**. The history of its clans is displayed at the **Glencoe Visitor Centre. On the A 82, in no time you reach the Highland capital** of Fort William → p. 65. From here you can head into the Nevis valley to catch a glimpse of the highest mountain, **⑯ Ben Nevis → p. 65. Now, it's a short journey to Skye → p. 80 – via the A 82 and A 87, and shortly before the island you will pass the Highlands' most photogenic image of Eilean Donan Castle.** Heading west on the **A 87, cross Skye Bridge and head on the A 855 for the picturesque town of ⑰ Portree → p. 80** to enjoy a coffee in the harbour. Just before Staffin you can check into the remote country hotel **⑱ The Glenview → p. 81** which has pleasant rooms and serves an excellent dinner.

You leave Skye from the ferry port of Uig and on the A 87, travelling across wonderful countryside via the A 890 and A 832 to the sub-tropical ⑲ Inverewe Gardens → p. 85. Here, you can go on a lengthy exploration tour with some sandwiches from the café. **Via the A 832 and A 835 head onto the remote spot of ⑳ Ullapool → p. 84**. At **The Ceilidh Place**, you can get something to eat, whisky, live music and a bed for the night.

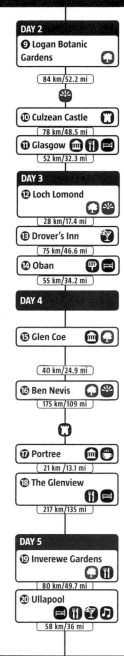

DAY 2

⑨ Logan Botanic Gardens

84 km/52.2 mi

⑩ Culzean Castle

78 km/48.5 mi

⑪ Glasgow

52 km/32.3 mi

DAY 3

⑫ Loch Lomond

28 km/17.4 mi

⑬ Drover's Inn

75 km/46.6 mi

⑭ Oban

55 km/34.2 mi

DAY 4

⑮ Glen Coe

40 km/24.9 mi

⑯ Ben Nevis

175 km/109 mi

⑰ Portree

21 km/13.1 mi

⑱ The Glenview

217 km/135 mi

DAY 5

⑲ Inverewe Gardens

80 km/49.7 mi

⑳ Ullapool

58 km/36 mi

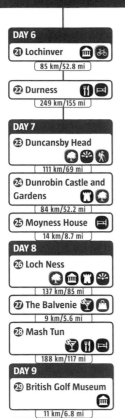

DAY 6

㉑ Lochinver

85 km/52.8 mi

㉒ Durness

249 km/155 mi

DAY 7

㉓ Duncansby Head

111 km/69 mi

㉔ Dunrobin Castle and Gardens

84 km/52.2 mi

㉕ Moyness House

14 km/8.7 mi

DAY 8

㉖ Loch Ness

137 km/85 mi

㉗ The Balvenie

9 km/5.6 mi

㉘ Mash Tun

188 km/117 mi

DAY 9

㉙ British Golf Museum

11 km/6.8 mi

㉚ The Peat Inn

73 km/45.4 mi

❶ Edinburgh

Travelling through the wild, deserted north-west, carry onto the A 835 and 837 to remote **㉑ Lochinver** → p. 85, where you collect bicycles hired from **The Rose Guest House** → p. 85. You can enjoy a four-hour cycle tour on the local routes. **Back on the A 894 and 838, you arrive near wonderful beaches at the village of ㉒ Durness** → p. 85. Cosy beds and wonderful food await at the first-class B & B **Mackay's**. Next day, along wonderful and deserted bays via the A 836 and 839 you reach the north-eastern headland at **㉓ Duncansby Head**: take a while to hike and enjoy the bird's-eye view! **Heading south on the coastal roads A 99 and A 9 you reach ㉔ Dunrobin Castle and Gardens** → p. 69. The stately home and gardens are ancient! **Back on the A 9 you soon arrive in busy Inverness** → p. 67, where you can stay overnight in **㉕ Moyness House**.

Take the A 82 to **㉖ Loch Ness** → p. 70 with the **Loch Ness Visitor Centre in Drumnadrochit,** where you can immerse yourself in the legends about Nessie. From **Urquhart Castle** → p. 70 take in the views across the lake. **Back in Inverness, head southwards on the A9, and via the A 938 and A 95 head for the whisky-producing, meandering riverside on Speyside as far as the malt capital of Duff-town** → p. 64. Enjoy a guided tour and the temptations of the distillery **㉗ The Balvenie**. **Then, follow the signs to the village Aberlour,** where you check in at the quaint whisky pub **㉘ Mash Tun** → p. 65. **Take the A 96 and A 90 via Dundee to the golf capital St Andrews** → p. 72, where you can learn all about the game in the **㉙ British Golf Museum**. Arrive for dinner at 7pm in the excellent **㉚ The Peat Inn** → p. 73 (booking essential!) in Cupar. It's only another hour back to **❶ Edinburgh** and the **Angel's Share Hotel** → p. 50.

❷ HIKING AROUND QUIRAING

START: ❶ Quiraing car park END: ❶ Quiraing car park	**3.5 hours** Actual walking time 3 hours
Distance: Medium difficulty 🕐 6.5 km/4 mi 📶 Height: 350 m/1148 ft	

WHAT TO PACK: Drinking water, sandwiches, sturdy hiking boots

IMPORTANT TIPS: A good fitness level is essential! The weather should be fine!

In the north of Skye, the Quiraing massive rock formation was formed by a landslip. A pass road winds its way through to a car park. Start here and head for the hiking trail, which is steep and rocky in parts, and has fantastic views.

It's probably Scotland's most spectacular mountain hiking trail: from ❶ **the car park at Quiraing** head northwards. **It's uphill from the start until after 500 m/1640 ft you have to cross a small stream running through a ravine.** You can already see your first destination ahead – a craggy, rectangular rock called ❷ **Prison**. Heading in an easterly direction, you follow a trail leading between Prison and a rock formation, the ❸ **Needle**. Take a break after about 1.5 km/0.9 mi between the rock faces and enjoy the views of the sea and moors.

Climb over a wire fence and follow a trail with the rock face on the left- and grassy slope on the right-hand side. Now, head downhill into a small valley. You will notice piles of stones as route markers – take the left-hand path leading along the rock face to a little wall that you climb over. Head downhill again to a fence that you also cross.

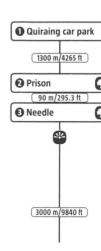

❶ Quiraing car park

1300 m/4265 ft

❷ Prison

90 m/295.3 ft

❸ Needle

3000 m/9840 ft

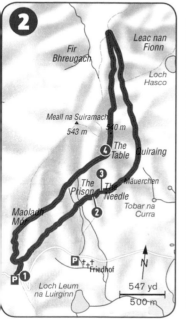

In fine weather, change plans to go hiking at Quiraing

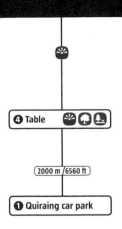

❹ Table

2000 m / 6560 ft

❶ Quiraing car park

Take a sharp left turn uphill, keeping close to the edge of a rock face if you feel dizzy. Staffin, the island of Raasay and the mountains of the mainland line up. You feel like you're on top of the world. Carry on uphill until after about 540 m/1772 ft you reach a grassy platform, which is surrounded by cliffs, and can only be viewed from above: the **❹ Table**. The views are rewarding after your scramble uphill over muddy peat. If it's not windy, this is the ▐INSIDER TIP▌ loveliest spot for a snack. **From here, follow the visible path downhill, through a gate in the fence, cross a grassy slope and you will notice the car park below.** It's a steep drop over grass, peat and rocks until you meet the ascending path again which you follow to the plateau of the pass road and the **❶ car park at Quiraing.**

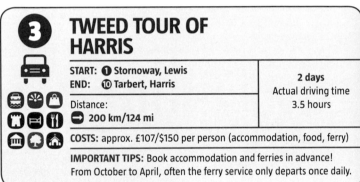

❸ TWEED TOUR OF HARRIS

START: ❶ Stornoway, Lewis **END: ❿ Tarbert, Harris**	**2 days** Actual driving time 3.5 hours
Distance: ➡ **200 km/124 mi**	
COSTS: approx. £107/$150 per person (accommodation, food, ferry)	

IMPORTANT TIPS: Book accommodation and ferries in advance! From October to April, often the ferry service only departs once daily.

For centuries, a familiar sound on the Outer Hebrides islands of Harris and Lewis in the Atlantic was the clatter of weaving looms. *Harris Tweed*, the weatherproof fabric made from wool, was manufactured here. After some years of decline, the fabric is back in fashion again. To see the enchanting countryside and its famous peaks, travel to the islands by car ferry and undertake a two-day round trip once you are here.

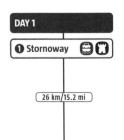

DAY 1

❶ Stornoway

26 km/15.2 mi

The Caledonian MacBrayne *(www.calmac.co.uk)* ferries transport passengers and cars several times a day in two-and-a-half hours from Ullapool to **❶ Stornoway** → p. 76 on the Isle of Lewis. The only eye-catching highlight during a short tour of the small port is **Lewis Castle**. It was built in the 19th century by a Scotsman who made his fortune from the opium trade. **North of Stornoway turn right and travel across Lewis on the A 857 in a westerly direction. Keep left along the coast road and take the A 858**

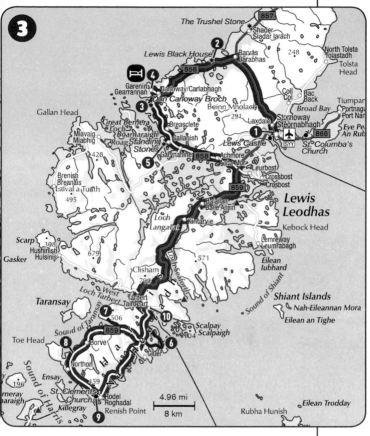

in a south-westerly direction to Arnol. Here, you will see the ruins of old farm cottages known as *blackhouses*. Visit the ❷ **Blackhouse Museum** *(April–Sept Mon–Sat 9.30am–5.30pm, Oct–March Mon, Tue, Thu, Fri 9.30am–4.30pm | £4.50)*. On show is the typical thatched cottage, which was deserted in 1966, and where the open indoor fires once covered the walls in soot – hence the term 'blackhouse'. **Head further southwards on the A858 across the coastal landscape dotted with moorland lakes as far as the village of Carloway** where you can climb the ❸ **Dun Carloway Broch**, the amazing ruin of a round tower house, about 2000 years old. There are far-reaching views from the old fortress. **Make a detour on the track heading north**

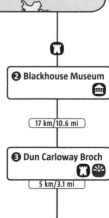

❷ Blackhouse Museum

17 km/10.6 mi

❸ Dun Carloway Broch

5 km/3.1 mi

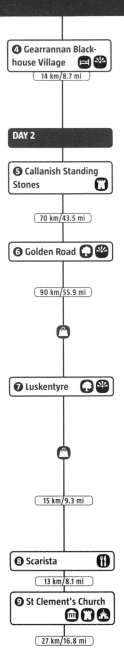

④ Gearrannan Black-house Village

14 km/8.7 mi

DAY 2

⑤ Callanish Standing Stones

70 km/43.5 mi

⑥ Golden Road

90 km/55.9 mi

⑦ Luskentyre

15 km/9.3 mi

⑧ Scarista

13 km/8.1 mi

⑨ St Clement's Church

27 km/16.8 mi

to **④ Gearrannan Blackhouse Village** → p. 79 by the sea. You can stop overnight in one of the cosy and fully refurbished self-catering farm cottages by the sea. From the hill behind the cottages you recognise the markings of the old fields and the beach – a typical sight of a crofting village with a fishing jetty.

Early in the morning head for Carloway and onto the A 858 travelling south. You will soon arrive at the most mystical place in the Hebrides: in the early daylight, you have the **⑤ Callanish Standing Stones** → p. 77, a 5000-year-old cult site, almost to yourself. **After travelling eastwards across the moor, you meet the A 859 and turn right. At Tarbert you can cross over to the mountainous neighbouring island of Harris which is connected with Lewis. After a further 5 km/3.1 mi, you turn left to the signposted ⑥ Golden Road** → p. 78, a narrow tarmac road along the rugged east coast – the views of the sea through the granite cliffs are austere but breathtakingly beautiful. You will come across tiny hamlets with Gaelic names like Plocropol, which seem entirely untouched by time, and where tweed looms still clatter. Signposts lead the way to small tweed shops. **After taking an about turn, you will arrive again on the A 859. Follow it in a southerly direction and then turn westwards on the same road; after about 6 km/3.7 mi turn right and head for 3 km/1.9 mi to the remote coastal town of ⑦ Luskentyre**. The panoramic vista of the fine sandy beach, clear water and glimmering granite mountains in the background is wonderful. A handful of houses reveal that people also live here. You can turn up unannounced at the home of the tweed weaver **INSIDER TIP ▶ Donald John Mackay**, who became world famous when the sports brand Nike ordered miles of tweed for a new range of sports shoe. **Turn back to the crossroads 4 km/2.5 mi away, heading south-west, and you will see the breathtaking scenery of this wild and romantic coastline.**

The most amazing stretch of beach is at the feet of the remote country hotel **⑧ Scarista** → p. 79, where you enjoy lunch. Rodel is then most likely the southern end of your tour. The tombstones of the clan chiefs are worthwhile seeing in the atmospheric **⑨ St Clement's Church**. If you want to continue your island tour further south and head for the island of North Uist, head over to Leverburgh. **On this tour, you are now heading back on the A 859 through the**

DISCOVERY TOURS

enchanting moon landscape along the east coast of Harris and back to ⑩ **Tarbert**, where after Uig you take the boat back to Skye.

④ THE HIGHLANDS BY TRAIN

START: ❶ Queen Street Station, Glasgow END: ⑪ Mallaig	3 days Actual driving time 12 hours
Distance: ➡ 300 km/186 mi	

COSTS: approx. £150/$210 per person (train tickets, accommodation, food)

IMPORTANT TIPS: ❹ **Corrour Station** is a request stop, please inform the conductor. Book accommodation/food in advance at ❺ **Corrour Station House Restaurant**.

A train journey across Scotland combines leisure and relaxing hours travelling in small carriages whilst admiring the moors, forests and mountain valleys. The tour takes three days with some spectacular stops along the way.

08:15am From ❶ **Glasgow's Queen Street Station** the West Highland Line departs several times daily for Fort William to Mallaig on the west coast. The train first follows the right bank of the River Clyde. After 20 minutes on the left you will notice the 1.3 km/0.8 mi long Erskine Bridge. For 10 km/6.2 mi images of industrial activity glide by the train. From Helensburgh, it heads in a northerly direction at Gare Loch and close to Loch Long on the left. Shortly after Arrochar before heading to Loch Lomond → p. 71, the countryside becomes mountainous on the left: the locals call this the Arrochar Alps. Minutes later the panorama of the legendary lake comes into view on the right. Shortly after 10am you reach ❷ **Ardlui** and disembark. **On the northern side of the station is the cosy Ardlui Hotel** with a fabulous view of the northern end of the loch. **You can buy a packed lunch here and take a short ferry ride (£3) to the other side of the lake where you can go hiking 500 m/1640 ft southwards on the ❸ West Highland Way** → **p. 108**. You can take in the panoramic views of the loch, forest and mountains over a picnic.

01:45pm Your train leaves Ardlui. The Highlands are now in view. Behind the Bridge of Orchy on the left is Loch Tully,

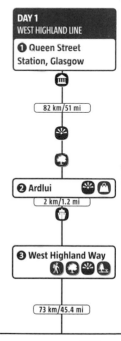

DAY 1
WEST HIGHLAND LINE

❶ Queen Street Station, Glasgow

82 km/51 mi

❷ Ardlui

2 km/1.2 mi

❸ West Highland Way

73 km/45.4 mi

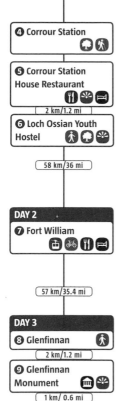

4 Corrour Station

5 Corrour Station House Restaurant

2 km/1.2 mi

6 Loch Ossian Youth Hostel

58 km/36 mi

DAY 2

7 Fort William

57 km/35.4 mi

DAY 3

8 Glenfinnan

2 km/1.2 mi

9 Glenfinnan Monument

1 km/0.6 mi

then the carriages rattle at a maximum of 48 km/h/ 30 mph through the barren and austere Rannoch Moor. At the heart of this peaceful spot is Britain's remotest and highest railway station (411 m/1348 ft): **4 Corrour Station → p. 66**, a must for hikers. At the station amidst the spectacular moorland is the appealing **5 Corrour Station House Restaurant** *(April–Oct | Budget)* with fine game dishes, a cosy fire and three rooms with views. Half an hour's walk after dinner takes you to the **6 Loch Ossian Youth Hostel → p. 66** – it was converted into an eco-hostel and has an idyllic location on the loch. Experienced long-distance runners can tackle the **INSIDER TIP Loch Ossian Challenge**, a solitary 12-km/7.5-mi run around the lake: the Hostel Warden logs your time and keeps the record list (since 1977).

08:45am The morning train takes about an hour to reach **7 Fort William → p. 65**, the top destination for mountain bikers. **Take a taxi to the outdoor centre Nevis Range** (bike.nevisrange.co.uk) where you can hire a mountain bike (from £22) and ride in the cable car uphill. You can take the rocky downhill trail, if you want to test your skill. Stay overnight at **The Lime Tree** in Fort William where you can enjoy an excellent dinner.

12:00pm About half an hour by train brings you to the village of **8 Glenfinnan** on Loch Shiel. The four-hour stop is enough for a 4-km/2.5-mi circular trail which includes climbing the solitary **9 Glenfinnan Monument** (£3.50) on the eastern side of the station. **Then continue for about**

Cinematic: Harry Potter's Hogwarts Express already steamed across Glenfinnan Viaduct

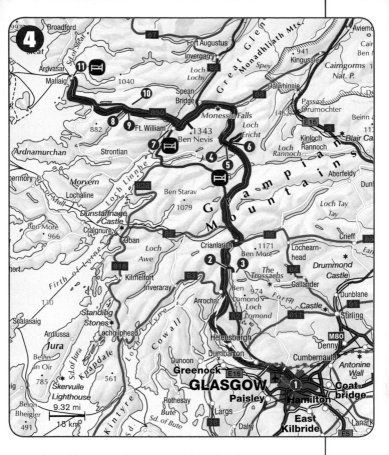

1 km/0.6 mi further north to the next high point above the 380-m/1247-ft long and 30-m/98.4-ft high ⑩ **Glenfinnan Viaduct** – Hogwarts Express in the Harry Potter films uses this winding rail track. The Jacobite Steam Train speeds across just before 3pm.

04:45pm Back in the train you continue the remaining hour of the journey and enjoy wonderful panoramic views. In the fishing village of ⑪ **Mallaig** → **p. 82** you reach the last stop at 5.43pm. From the **West Highland Hotel** (20 rooms | tel. 01687 46 22 10 | Moderate) you have a wonderful sea view over dinner and can enjoy a short stroll in the busy fishing port.

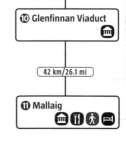

⑩ Glenfinnan Viaduct

42 km/26.1 mi

⑪ Mallaig

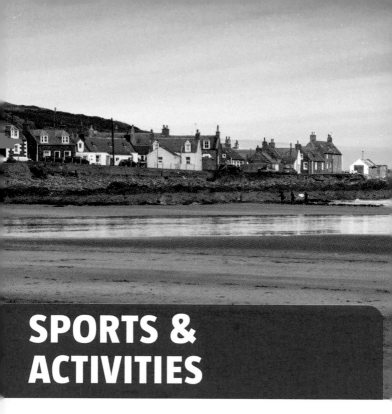

SPORTS & ACTIVITIES

Golf is a hugely popular sport in Scotland. The prices are reasonable so holidaymakers, even beginners, can try their hand at a round while the splendid coasts also draw novice sailors who want to see Scotland from a different perspective.

Be sure to pack your hiking boots for the Highlands and the glens, and you may even want to hire a mountain bike for a cross-country cycle. The countless lakes and rivers are great for anglers and canoers. Outdoor centres offer plenty of sports activities like at Great Glen Water Park *(South Laggan, near Spean Bridge | greatglenwaterpark.co.uk)*. Nature expeditions are the Scots' idea of wellness offers. The wonderful spa hotels focus on massages, manicures and poolside relaxation *(www.spabreak.co.uk/Scotland)*.

ANGLING

Scotland offers world-class fishing so it is 'tight lines!' on just about all the rivers and lakes. Visitors can enquire at local tourist offices about day licences and they are generally obtainable from the post office or angling clubs. As a rule the fee is around £5 per day for fish such as pike or carp but if it's salmon you're after then spots on the best rivers can command as much as over £400. Country hotels often offer their guests free fishing opportunities. Trout fishing is possible between March and October, while the salmon season is from January to October. Famous salmon rivers are the Tweed, Spey and Dee, while the many larger Highland

Hiking, fishing, golf and sailing:
there are many ways to best experience
Scotland's nature

lochs are top trout areas: *www.fishing scotland.net*

CANOEING & KAYAKING

Countless rivers, 6000 lakes and thousands of miles of coast make for the perfect terrain for both beginner and experienced canoeists. Water sports centres such as *Elie Watersports (Fife | tel. 01333 33 09 62 | www.eliewater sports.com)* in the small town by the same name and *Croft-na-Caber (Loch* *Tay | tel. 01887 83 05 88)* offer courses and boats. The west coast and the Outer Hebrides coastline are particularly recommended – the latter is listed as one of the world's best sea kayaking areas *(short.travel/scot10)*. Try *Uist Outdoor Centre (Lochmaddy, | tel. 01876 50 04 80 | www.uistoutdoorcentre.co.uk)* for good equipment and guides, also for beginners. From here you can also get INSIDER TIP sea kayak transport to the remote St Kilda archipelago. A tip for beginners: *Dun Eadinn Sea Kayaking* at the Firth of Forth near Edinburgh offers manageable sea kayaking excursions. You will kayak beneath the famous red railway bridge and to the islands in the Forth. The route is rich in bird and seal life. *From 3 hours and £45 | tel. 07786 510771 (mobile) | www.duneideannsea kayaking.com*

CYCLING

The quiet and well demarcated cycling routes of the Borders region are perfect for some tranquil – if occasionally hilly – bicycle outings. The *4 Abbeys Cycle Route* links all the abbey ruins in a 90 km/55.9 mi round trip while the *Tweed Cycle Way* explores the Borders east coast on a 145 km/90 mi stretch from Biggar to Berwick-upon-Tweed *(www.cyclescottishborders.com)*. The well marked *Great Glen Cycle Route* goes 130 km/81 mi from Fort William to Inverness. Information on long distance cycling routes: *www.cycle-n-sleep.co.uk*. Best for mountain biking is *Leanachan Forest* in the Nevis range. Further information: *short.travel/scot18*

DIVING

Dive enthusiasts can rent the necessary equipment from dive centres and many also offer courses. Experienced divers will appreciate the spectacular dive off Stromness where INSIDER TIP German shipwrecks from World War I are 50 m/164 ft deep in the Scapa Flow: *see p. 90*. The good underwater visibility around the Outer Hebrides, such as North Uist or at the Summer Isles off Ullapool, are also ideal conditions for beginners. St Abb's Head near Eyemouth on the east coast is a *marine reserve* which means there is plenty of underwater life here *(www.divestay.co.uk)*.

GOLF

There are more than 500 golf courses and even on the remotest islands you can spend time on the local green from around £20. Golf clubs are all open to the general public. For beginners the best options are Scotland's numerous golfing hotels – and it doesn't have to be the famous *Gleneagles* in Perthshire the first time round. Seasoned players who want to tee off on sought after greens like *St Andrews* or *Troon* will be paying £250 upwards and should book months in advance.

In the country that invented golf, there are breathtaking courses where the spectacular countryside is a distraction from teeing off: in the north is the famous links course at Balnakeil Bay *(from £20 | www.durnessgolfclub.org)*, on Orkney you can play a round at the legendary Scapa Flow *(from £25 | www.strom nessgc.co.uk)*. On Harris you can attempt nine holes close to the location where the acclaimed film director Stanley Kubrick once shot the sci-fi classic "2001" *(from £20 in honesty box | www.harris golf.com)*. More information: *www.golf. visitscotland.com*

HIKING

The ★ *West Highland Way* (www. west-highland-way.co.uk) (152 km/94 mi) from Milngavie (Glasgow) to Ben Nevis at Fort William is ideal because it is well signposted and feasible without a tent. The *Southern Upland Way (www.southern uplandway.gov.uk)* (350 km/217 mi) connects Portpatrick in the south of the west coast with St Bathans on the east coast. The climb up and down Ben Nevis from Fort William takes a day. The Hebridean island of Skye has superb hiking terrain: easy trails through the moors, strenuous hill walks and challenging climbs in the breathtaking Cuillins Mountains. Organised hikes in small groups are offered by *Walk About Scotland (April–Oct | tel. 0131 2 43 26 64 (*) | www.walkaboutscotland.com)*. A weekend trip from Edinburgh is well worth

SAILING, SURFING & WINDSURFING

The waters between the Inner Hebrides and around Skye make for challenging sailing areas. From Rothesay on the Isle of Bute you can take leisurely day or

Distinctive landscapes, magical lighting effects: hiking on the Isle of Skye

it (from £195). Week-long trips with set dates to an island such as Skye cost from £1025 including meals, guided tour, accommodation and transport.

HORSEBACK RIDING

Discover Scotland at a gallop! Whether you want to trek across rivers, into the mountains or at sunset along the beach: the country offers options for every style of horseback riding. In the north you can try *Highlands Unbridled (Tain | tel. 01862 7350 07 | www.highlandsunbridled.co.uk)* while *Tomintoul Riding Centre (St Bridget Farm | Ballindalloch | tel. 01807 58 02 10 | www.highlandhooves.co.uk)* covers the Malt Whisky Trail and the Cairngorms National Park. Certified horseback riding clubs: *www.ridingin scotland.com/centres*

weekly trips organised by the *Bute Sailing School | Battery Place | Rothesay | tel. 01700 50 48 81*. For information about charters and sailing lessons go to *www.sailscotland.co.uk*.

A good spot for windsurfing and dinghy sailing beginners is Loch Lomond; for the more experienced the west coast is recommended. You can take a one week sailing course with *Tighnabruaich Sailing School (Tighnabruaich | Argyll | tel. 01700 81 17 17 | www.tssargyll.co.uk)*. The conditions at the Mull of Kintyre in Machrihanish and on Lewis are excellent for surfers: *Hebridean Surf (Stornoway | tel. 01851 84 03 43 | www.hebrideansurf.co.uk)*, while the Isle of Tiree – daily by ferry or air *(Loganair)* – has Scotland's best windsurfing conditions. General information on sailing: *www.sailscotland.co.uk*

TRAVEL WITH KIDS

Scotland with the kids? It's a must. The adventure parks, clearly signposted nature trails starting from Highland car parks offer plenty of thrills. The boat trips and colonies of seabirds are unforgettable. And the chips are homemade ...

CREAM O'GALLOWAY 🌱
(125 F5) (*ᶆ J15*)
This farm near Rainton in the Galloway region makes delicious ice cream from organic milk. With a huge serving in hand, your children can first view the cattle and sheep enclosures and then amuse themselves in the adventure park which has a high tower that looks across to the Isle of Man. *March–Oct 10am–6pm | near Rainton, south of Gatehouse of Fleet, between Dumfries and Stranraer | www.creamogalloway.co.uk*

DEEP SEA WORLD (126 C1) (*f K12*)
In an old quarry beneath the wonderful Forth Rail Bridge near Edinburgh is the world's longest underwater tunnel – see seals, rays and colourful fish and from the café you can watch the divers feed the sharks. Tip: book online! *Mon–Fri 10am–5pm, Sat–Sun 10am–6pm | children £11, from the age of 13 years £15 |* *North Queensferry | 15 minutes by train with the Fife Circle Line from Edinburgh | www.deepseaworld.com*

HAUNTED TOURS (131 D6) (*ᶆ L12*)
Everyone is bound to get goose bumps on one of the *Auld Reekie Tours (daily from noon | adults from £10, children from £8 | 45 Niddry St. | tel. 0131 5 57 47 00 | www.auldreekietours.com)* such as the evening walks through the alleyways of Edinburgh or a tour of the places where witches gathered or of creepy underground vaults. The most informative – and least gruesome – tour takes you on an hour-long walk through the secret warren of streets below the Royal Mile that were closed off because of the plague: *The Real Mary King's Close (daily 10am–5pm | children £9, from 15 years £14.75 | 2 Warriston's Close | www.realmarykingsclose.com)*

KELBURN CASTLE (125 D2) (*ᶆ H13*)
A castle surrounded by a mysterious forest with hiking trails and wild flowing waters. The guided pony rides are a hit with children as is their custom built indoor play area in a wooden fort with slides etc. Appealing wall murals cover the southern side of the old walls. *Daily from*

The land of castles, ghosts, seals, puffins and dolphins: Scotland is one big adventure playground

Easter to end Oct 10am–6pm | adults £9, children £7 | family glamping: tel. 01475 56 86 85 | Largs (A78) | www.kelburnestate.com

INSIDER TIP LEAULT FARM ●
(130 B1) *(∅ J8)*

Scottish Border Collies are made to guard sheep (as well as ducks and their masters). Shepherds used to look after their Highland sheep with the smart dogs that they attracted with whistles and calls. You can watch this fascinating spectacle at 4pm (45 minutes, no prior booking) at the Leault Highland Farm near Kincraig. Neil Ross also gives general tips for handling dogs. *June–Oct daily except Sat | Kincraig near Aviemore | Exit from the B 9152 | tel. 01540 65 14 02 | www.leault workingsheepdogs.co.uk*

MUSEUM OF CHILDHOOD
(131 D6) *(∅ L12)*

The museum is crammed with toys and the dolls, tin soldiers, old books and model trains are so interesting that you and your children will not want to leave. *Mon–Sat 10am–5pm, July/Aug also Sun noon–5pm | admission free | 42 High Street | Edinburgh*

WILDLIFE

Puffins, cormorants, dolphins and seals: the best time to watch the wildlife along Scotland's coast is from May to July. Hiking across the Isle of Handa off Scotland's north-west coast is a memorable experience for both children and adults. 100,000 seabirds brood here *(ferry April–Aug Mon–Sat 9.30am–5pm | children £5, from 15 years £13 | tel. 07780 96 78 00 | www.handa-ferry.com)*. Great bird watching sites are also *Fowlsheugh Reserve* at Stonehaven/Aberdeenshire, the cliffs of *Papa Westray* on Orkney Mainland, *Sumburgh Head,* the *Isle of Noss* on the Shetland Islands, the *Scottish Seabird Centre* in North Berwick and *Bass Rock* island in the south-east. Info: *www.wild scotland.org.uk*

FESTIVALS & EVENTS

Scotland loves festivals! The most important celebrations are the Highland Games, 'Scotland's Olympic Games' countrywide from June to September, and the numerous folk festivals are also popular: www.scottish-folk-music.com. Edinburgh even has 20 festivals: *www.edinburghspotlight.com*

FESTIVALS & LOCAL EVENTS

JANUARY
Celtic Connection festival in Glasgow. *www.celticconnections.com*
Burns Supper is celebrated in pubs and restaurants around the country with haggis, whisky and poetry to commemorate the birthday of poet Robert Burns (25 January)
Up Helly Aa is a pretty wild fire festival, which is held in Lerwick, Shetland and ends with the ceremonial burning of a Viking boat

APRIL
Edinburgh International Science Festival www.sciencefestival.co.uk

MAY
● *Shetland Folk Festival* is a non-profit festival; *www.shetlandfolkfestival.com*

● *Orkney Folk Festival* www.orkneyfolkfestival.com
Blair Atholl Highlands Gathering with a parade by the Atholl Highlanders – Scotland's only private army. *www.blairatholl.org.uk*
Edinburgh Marathon is the UK's second-largest distance run with more than 30,000 participants. *www.edinburghmarathon.com*

JUNE
INSIDER TIP **St Magnus Festival** on Mainland Orkney is a week-long festival celebrating classical music and Scottish literature. *www.stmagnusfestival.com*
Royal Highland Show in Edinburgh is Scotland's largest agricultural show
Edinburgh Festival of Cycling

JUNE–AUGUST
INSIDER TIP **Common Ridings** take place in 11 Borders towns: a combination of riding festival, music parade and fair commemorating the tradition of clan boundary riding. *www.returntotheridings.co.uk*

JULY
Hebridean Celtic Music Festival is a famous folk festival in Stornoway. *www.hebceltfest.com*

The Scots loves celebrating: tips on where to see caber tossing, where the whisky flows – and when summer transforms a city to one big festival

Herring Queen Festival is held in Eyemouth

AUGUST

★ *Mad Edinburgh* In August, the city comes alive with 2 million visitors flocking to celebrate the festival. A must for dedicated fans is the *Edinburgh International Festival (www.eif.co.uk)*: held since 1947, it involves three weeks of concerts and theatre with many international stars. *The Fringe (www.edfringe.com)* is the world's biggest cultural festival and a celebration of every imaginable contemporary and experimental art form. Taking place at the same time is the world-famous *Military Tattoo*, the *International Book Festival* and the *Just Festival (just-festival.org)* for humanity. *www.edinburghfestivalcity.com*
The *Alternative Games* in Parton have revived snail racing and a tractor show.

SEPTEMBER

★ ● *Highland Games* in Braemar. Traditional event attended by the royal family with disciplines that range from the caber toss to bagpipe competitions. *www.braemargathering.org*

PUBLIC HOLIDAYS

1 Jan	New Year's Day
2 Jan	Bank Holiday (Banks and public institutions are closed)
March/April	Good Friday
first and last Mon in May	Bank Holiday
first or last Mon in Aug	Bank Holiday
25/26 Dec	Christmas Day, Boxing Day

LINKS, BLOGS, APPS & MORE

www.guardian.com/edinburgh Topical current affairs contributions about Edinburgh and Scotland, from England's best newspaper

www.nts.org.uk/ThistleCamps If you are a nature lover and don't mind getting your hands dirty then grab a spade and help the non-profit National Trust of Scotland. They offer working holidays on more than 100 properties. You can make a contribution by taking care of the natural environment. So how about gardening and sheep shearing on Fair Isle or doing some drystone walling in Glencoe?

www.edinburghwhiskyblog.com A quirky blog run by two twentysomething whisky connoisseurs from Edinburgh who call themselves 'spirit geeks'! A blog that is a breath of fresh air in the malt world

www.undiscoveredscotland.co.uk An excellent and well-resourced online guide that not only offers information about travel destinations, but also gives tips on medical care where you are staying

short.travel/scot19 Are you travelling by boat? You can look up the tidal times here

www.mwis.org.uk/scottish-forecast Scottish weather is very changeable. The regional forecast is very helpful if you are planning a mountain hike

short.travel/scot14 Renting a private apartment in Edinburgh is made easier because the locals prefer to get away during the fes-

Regardless of whether you are still reasearching your trip or already in Scotland: these addresses will provide you with more information, videos and networks to make your holiday even more enjoyable

tival months. Glasgow also offers some attractive private residences

short.travel/scot4 A home exchange site where you can swap your own home for a stay in say, a penthouse in Glasgow, or an apartment on Skye. There are a number of listings for each area in Scotland

short.travel/scot2 In just eight minutes you learn a whole lot about the history and production of the Scottish national drink

VIDEOS & MUSIC

short.travel/scot5 An interesting video about a falconer in the Highlands

short.travel/scot3 A short film about the training of Scottish sheep Border collies, it clearly demonstrates their remarkable instinct for herding and driving

short.travel/scot20 Informative film about the classical music festival 'Mendelssohn on Mull'

APPS

Cairngorms National Park – GPS Map Navigator The nature reserve's own app gives you up to date information on the weather in the mountains, restaurants and accommodation in addition to detailed route maps for motorists and hikers. It can also help you track down last minute offers if you need somewhere to stay

iFringe The new App (annually updated) for the world's biggest cultural festival in Edinburgh

Ian Rankin's Edinburgh With this free app you can join the crime thriller author on a personal tour of the city of Edinburgh – it includes audio and video extras. Rankin's protagonist, Inspector John Rebus, also features

NorthCoast500 An excellent guide for planning and taking with you on the new 830-km/516-mi stretch of the hiking route around the North Highlands

TRAVEL TIPS

ACCOMMODATION

Scotland offers a wide range of accommodation options. If you like the idea of a holiday apartment in a castle or an old, historical house then your best bet is the National Trust *(tel. 0131 458 03 05 | www.nts.org.uk)*. You can find select B&Bs listed at *www.scotlandsbestbandbs.co.uk*. For general accommodation and hotels a good website is *www.visitscotland.com*

If a farm holiday is what you are after then refer to *www.farmstay.co.uk/Places-ToVisit/Scotland*

ARRIVAL

✈ Scotland has four international airports; Edinburgh, Glasgow, Glasgow Prestwick and Aberdeen. There are direct flights to Scotland from the USA and Canada but those flying in from other countries will need to fly first to London or one of the other European hubs and then take a connecting flight. *Edinburgh Airport (www.edinburghairport.com)* is 12 km/7.5 mi west of the city centre. The tram ride to (www.edinburghtrams.com) Princes Street costs £5.50, the express bus no. 100 (www.lothianbuses.com) costs £4.50. You purchase the tickets at machines at the bus stops. A city day ticket for bus and tram costs £4, a single ticket costs £1.60. You can expect to pay about £20 for a taxi into the city. *Glasgow Prestwick Airport* is about 50 km/31.1 mi west of the city centre. Both the bus and train take about an hour to get into town *(£7–£14)*.

🚢 There are direct routes to Scottish ports from Northern Ireland and Ireland and indirect routes from Europe via Hull or Newcastle, in north-east England. From Northern Ireland, several companies run regular services (up to 8 times a day) between the Emerald Isle and Scotland. The routes between Belfast and Stranraer (a 2 hour crossing), Belfast and Cairnryan (2 hours 15 minutes) and Larne to Troon (2 hours) are probably the most interesting. For more information on routes and ticket prices: *Stena Line (www.stenaline.co.uk), P&O Ferries (www.poferries.com), DFDS Seaways (www.dfdsseaways.co.uk)* and *Irish Ferries (www.irishferries.com)*.

🚆 There are frequent direct train services from Kings Cross Station in London (every hour) to Edinburgh *(www.mytrainticket.co.uk)*. The journey usually takes around 4 hours and ticket prices vary from £20 to £200, depending on fare. The Glasgow service runs from London Euston and takes about 5 hours. *First ScotRail (www.firstscotrail.com)* also

RESPONSIBLE TRAVEL

It doesn't take a lot to be environmentally friendly whilst travelling. Don't just think about your carbon footprint whilst flying to and from your holiday destination but also about how you can protect nature and culture abroad. As a tourist it is especially important to respect nature, look out for local products, cycle instead of driving, save water and much more. If you would like to find out more about eco-tourism please visit: *www.ecotourism.org*

offer an overnight service, the *Caledonian Sleeper* from London Euston to Edinburgh, Glasgow, Stirling, Perth, Dundee, Aberdeen and Inverness. It is advisable to book your train travel to Scotland well in advance.

BANKS & CREDIT CARDS

You can withdraw cash using your EC or debit card at ATMs at the airport and at many locations in the city. Hotels, shops and restaurants will accept the standard credit cards, as will most of the pubs. Banks are open from *9am to 5pm Mon–Fri*, except, of course, on public holidays.

BUS

The bus companies *National Express* and *Scottish Citylink* cover an extensive network. If you're thinking of taking the bus frequently then you should enquire about specials at: *Scottish Citylink Coaches Ltd (tel. 0871 2 66 33 33 (*) | www.citylink.co.uk)*

CAMPING

Scotland has more than 500 camp sites. If you're travelling by camper van your best bet is to stay in a holiday park overnight. They usually also have stationary caravans for hire. For information on sites and prices go to: *short.travel/scot21*.

If you want to hire a camper you'll find top of the range models as well as budget options at: *www.coolcampervans.com*. Sites with high quality amenities are given the *Scottish Thistle Award*,

which is a tourism commendation for excellence. Camping out in the wild is not prohibited in Scotland but it is, of course, important that you ask permission from the landowner first. If you're thinking of parking your car or camper van somewhere on the side of the road, you should first make sure that there are not signs prohibiting this.

BUDGETING

Whisky	from £36/$50
	a bottle
Coffee	£2.20/$3
	a cup
Taxi	£8/$11
	for a short trip
Fish & Chips	£5.50/$7.50
	from a take-away
Petrol (gas)	£1.20/$1.60
	for a litre of regular
Soup	£4.50/$6
	in a pub

CLIMATE & WHEN TO GO

Scottish summers are usually quite mild with average temperature of around 21 °C/70 °F degrees. The mercury will seldom rise to more than 30 °C/86 °F and seldom drops below 14 °C/57 °F. In spring and autumn you can expect cool 10 °C/50 °F degree days. Scottish winters can be cold and rainy although temperatures below zero are rare, the Highlands are the exception. Always include warm and rainproof clothing when you pack.

CONSULATES & EMBASSIES

CONSULATE OF THE UNITED STATES OF AMERICA

3 Regent Terrace | Edinburgh EH7 5BW | tel. +44 13 15 56 83 51 | www.edinburgh.usconsulate.gov

AUSTRALIAN HONORARY CONSULATE

Mitchell House | 5 Mitchell Street | Edinburgh EH6 7DB | tel. +44 13 15 38 05 82 | www.dfat.gov.au/missions/countries/uked.html

CONSULATE OF CANADA

50 Lothian Road | Edinburgh EH3 9WJ | tel. +44 13 14 73 63 20 www.canadainternational.gc.ca/united_ kingdom

CUSTOMS

UK citizens do not have to pay any duty on goods brought from another EU country as long as tax was included in the price and the items are for private consumption only. Tax free allowances include: 800 cigarettes, 400 small cigars, 200 cigars, 1kg/2.2lbs pipe tobacco, 10L spirits, 20L liqueurs, 90L wine, 110L beer.

Those travelling from the USA, Canada, Australia or other non-EU countries are allowed to enter with the following tax-free amounts: 200 cigarettes or 100 small cigars or 50 cigars or 250g pipe tobacco. 2L wine and spirits with less than 22 vol. % alcohol, 1L spirits with more than 22 vol. % alcohol content.

American passport holders returning to the USA do not have to pay duty on articles purchased overseas up to the value of $800, but there are limits on the amount of alcoholic beverages and tobacco products. For regulations for international travel for U.S. residents see *www.cbp.gov*.

DRIVING IN SCOTLAND

Scotland has a well-developed road network and for tourists from outside of the UK: remember that you drive on the left in the UK. At roundabouts (which are everywhere in Britain) cars coming from the right have the right of way. The speed limit in built-up areas is 30 mph (48 km/h), 60 mph (97 km/h) on unrestricted single carriage roads and 70 mph (113 km/h) on motorways and dual carriageways. Filling stations on the islands and in the Highlands may be closed on a Sunday. Many of the roads on the islands and in the remote Highlands and coastal regions are single track with lay-bys to allow you to pull over to give way to oncoming traffic. An oncoming vehicle will flash their lights to let you know you are being given the right of way.

It costs about £25–£65 a day to hire a car (a valid credit card is required and the minimum age is 21 years). Both Edinburgh and Glasgow airports have several international car hire companies to choose from.

ELECTRICITY

220–240 volts AC. Three-pronged plugs are the norm so you may require an adapter. If you need one they are for sale in many places in Scotland or you can ask at your hotel.

EMERGENCY

Fire brigade, ambulance: *tel. 999*, police tel. *101*

EVENTS

The daily newspaper 'The Scotsman' *(www.scotsman.com)* publishes the dates and prices for many shows and events. The leading internet entertainment guide is 'The List' *(www.list.co.uk)* or you can go to the national portal *www.ticketmaster.co.uk* (type in Edinburgh in the search field).

FERRIES

The *Caledonian MacBrayne (tel. 0800 06650000 | www.calmac.co.uk)* transports passengers, bicycles and motor vehicles to the Inner and Outer Hebrides off the west coast. In the summer months it is advisable to book your trip in advance. *North Link Ferries (www.north linkferries.co.uk)* connects the mainland with Orkney and Shetland on the Scrabster–Stromness and Aberdeen–Kirwall–Lerwick routes.

HEALTH

For non-UK residents, the European insurance card *EHIC (European Health Insurance Card)* will be accepted by hospitals run by the *National Health Service (NHS)* and most doctors. In other cases you will have to pay directly and submit your bill for refunding when you return home.

IMMIGRATION

Citizens of the UK & Ireland, USA, Canada, Australia and New Zealand need only a valid passport to enter all countries of the EU. Children below the age of 12 need a children's passport. Check online for the latest travel advice and entry requirements: *www.gov.uk/foreign-travel-advice* (UK Citizens) or *www.state.gov/travel* (US Citizens)

INFORMATION

VISITSCOTLAND
General travel information *www.visitscotland.com*

INFORMATION IN EDINBURGH
Edinburgh iCentre | 3 Princes Street | Edinburgh EH2 2QP | tel. 0131 4 73 38 68 (*)

CURRENCY CONVERTER

US$	GBP	GBP	US$
1	0.75	10	13.50
2	1.50	20	27.00
3	2.25	25	33.75
4	3.00	30	40.50
5	3.75	40	54.00
6	4.50	50	67.50
7	5.25	70	94.50
8	6.00	80	108.00
9	6.75	95	128.25

NEWSPAPERS

The Scottish are very supportive of their own newspapers. In Edinburgh the leading newspaper is 'The Scotsman', in Glasgow it is 'The Glasgow Herald'. Major international newspapers are also available but not always on the day of publication.

OPENING TIMES

Most shops are open Mon–Sat 9am–5.30pm. The larger cities often offer extended shopping hours on Thursday and are sometimes also open on Sundays. Pubs are generally open until 11pm, post offices Mon–Fri 9am–5.30pm, the larger ones also on Saturdays from 9am–12.30pm.

PHONE & MOBILE PHONE

Dialling code to phone the UK from abroad: *+44;* from the UK to: United States and Canada *+1;* Ireland *+353;* Australia *+61*
Information: national *tel. 118500;* international: *tel. 118505.*

Caerlaverock Castle

Phone cards (values: £2–£20) can be purchased at the post office and in shops displaying the BT (British Telecom) symbol. Many phone booths will also accept standard credit cards.

Since the EU stopped high roaming charges, outgoing and ingoing calls on mobile phones are not as expensive. If you want to keep costs to a minimum, however, it is best to buy a pre-paid card from the supermarket.

PRICES & BANKNOTES

The Scots have their own currency, the Scottish pound which is the same value as the British pound sterling (see p. 25) there are 5, 10, 20 and 50 pound notes and uniquely in Scotland also a 1 pound note.

RAIL

Scotland by rail is an attractive alternative because of its scenic landscapes. You can book the *Brit Rail Scottish Freedom Pass* (four or eight days) online at *www.britrail. com* and timetables and routes at *www. scotrail.com*. It is easy to travel by train in Scotland, the trains travel from Edinburgh along the east coast, through central Scotland and further on all the way up to the ferries to Orkney. The train journey between Edinburgh and Glasgow only takes 50 minutes. From Glasgow you can travel on a very scenic route through Rannoch Moor to Fort William and the Isle of Skye. From Lochalsh on Skye the railway track traverses the Highlands to Inverness. The single carriage wagons generally have a first class section where you will be served coffee free of charge.

SWIMMING

Despite the breathtakingly beautiful and mostly deserted beaches, Scotland is not a beach holiday destination. The water temperature is rarely above 15 °C/59 °F. Anyone who wants to brave the beaches can find out more information about designated beaches for swimming from the environmental agency: short.travel/scot9.

TIME

Great Britain is on GMT, *Greenwich Mean Time*. The North American east coast is 5 hours behind, the west coast 8 hours.

TIPPING

As a rule in Scotland tips are included in the bill. Nevertheless, hotel staff and chambermaids will be appreciative of a small gratuity of say £1 or £2. In restaurants the menu usually states whether or not service is included. If you're happy with the service you should round up by 10 per cent for a tip. The same goes for taxi drivers.

TRAVEL CONCESSIONS

The Explorer Pass from Historic Scotland offers free entry to state attractions and discounts such as for the audio guides in

Edinburgh Castle. In addition it saves you having to queue in ticket lines. Historic Scotland is the authority for the conservation of the country's monuments and manages some 360 historical sites such as fortresses, castles and dream destinations like Skara Brae on Orkney. There are two variations of the pass: the three-day pass (£23.20) which can be used within a period of five days and the seven-day pass (£30.40) which is valid for a period of 14 days. There are also inexpensive family passes (£60.80) that are valid from the first time you use them. For information and to buy online go to: *www.historic-scotland.gov.uk/explorer.htm*

WEIGHTS & MEASURES

Officially Scotland and Great Britain use the metric and decimal system but the imperial standards are still in use in everyday life:

1 inch = 2.54 cm; 1 foot = 30.48 cm; 1 yard = 91.44 cm; 1 mile = 1.609 km; 1 ounce = 28.35 g; 1 pound = 453.59 g; 1 pint = 0.5683 l; 1 Imp. gal = 1.2 US liq gal = 4.5459 l.

WIFI & INTERNET

In hotels and many B&Bs you generally have access to free Wi-Fi. Cafés and bars also offer wireless Internet. The use of prepaid hourly or daily hotspots is less frequent.

YOUTH HOSTELS

Many of the youth hostels are in the Highlands, especially in areas popular for sports and activities. You need to be a member of the Scottish Youth Hostels Association and you can apply for this when you arrive. Information: *SYHA National Office | 7 Glebe Crescent | Stirling FK82JA | tel. 01786 89 14 00 | www.syha.org.uk*

WEATHER IN EDINBURGH

	Jan	Feb	March	April	May	June	July	Aug	Sept	Oct	Nov	Dec
Daytime temperatures in °C/°F	6/43	6/43	8/46	11/52	14/57	17/63	18/64	18/64	16/61	12/54	9/48	7/45
Nighttime temperatures in °C/°F	1/34	1/34	2/36	4/39	6/43	9/48	11/52	11/52	9/48	7/45	4/39	2/36
☀ Sunshine hours/day	2	3	3	5	6	6	5	4	4	3	2	2
☂ Precipitation days/month	13	11	11	11	11	12	13	13	12	13	12	13

ROAD ATLAS

The green line indicates the Discovery Tour 'Scotland at a glance'
The blue line indicates the other Discovery Tours

All tours are also marked on the pull-out map

Photo: Kelso, River Tweed

Exploring Scotland

**The map on the back cover shows how
the area has been sub-divided**

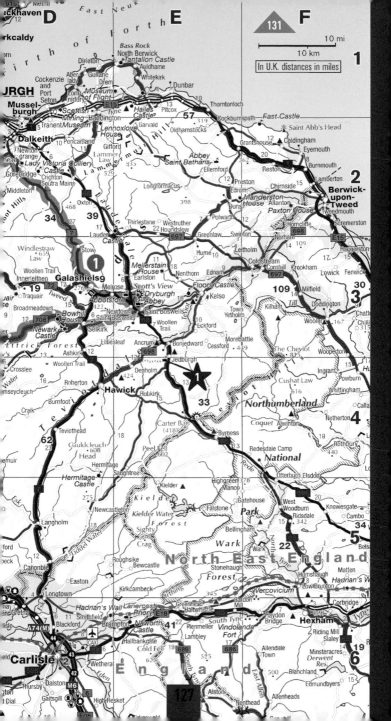

Skye

Idrigill Point Wiay
Fiskavaig

Peinchorran Sconser Scalpay Kyle of L
Crofters Museum Pabay Ky
House Hou

Merkadale Drynoch
Talisker Distillery Sligachan Hotel

M a n g - i n - i s h Luib Broadford

Cuillin Hills Loch Torrin Skula

Glenbrittle Sgurr Coruisk 851
House 993 14
Alasdair Loch
Slapin Isle

Soay Loch
Elgol 299 17

Prince Charles's
Cave Knock
Castle

Magnetic Hill Armadale
Castle &
Canna Clan Donald
Centre

Sanday Aird of Sleat
Sound of Canna Point of Sleat M

A'Bhrideanach Kinloch Castle
Askival Glenancross
Rum 812 Bunacaimb 10 Aris
Rhum
Sound of Rhum Cleadale Eigg 994

Rubh' Arisaig

Muck Sound
of Arisaig

Castlebay Eilean
Shona
Ockle Ardtoe Ac

Point of Achosnich A r d n a m u r c h a n Salen
Ardnamurchan Glenborrodale 861
528 23 512 Carna
Kilchoan
Sorisdale Oronsay Canr

Arnabost Tobermory Drimnin
Ballyhaugh Arinagour
Arileod Caliach Point M o r
Coll Calgary Dervaig 550
10
Caoles Achleck
Clachan Mor 5 Loch Tuath 33
6 4 Scarinish Treshnish Islands 424 Salen 849
Barrapol 1 Crossapol Gometra 313 Fishnish Du
41 Tiree Gha
Staffa Ulva Loch na Keal 766
Fingal's Cave 10 Inchkenneth Balnahard Ben More 18
Chapel M u l l
Ardmeanach Lochbuie
The Burgh
Abbey Loch Scridain 849
Iona 101 Fionnphort 20 376 Carsaig 405
Baile Mor Bunessan Mull Carsaig Bay
Benedictine Ross Carsaig Arches Fi
Nunnery Erraid
Garvella

Kiloran 43
Gardens
Colonsay Scalasaig J u r a

10 mi

10 km

In U.K. distances in miles

Oronsay Port Askaig Rubh 477 846
a' Mhail Loch Tarbe

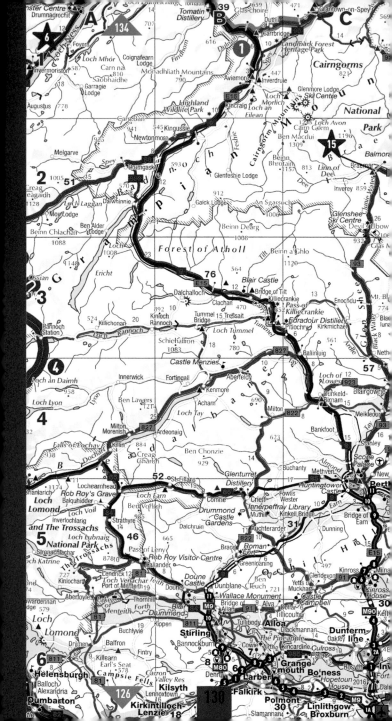

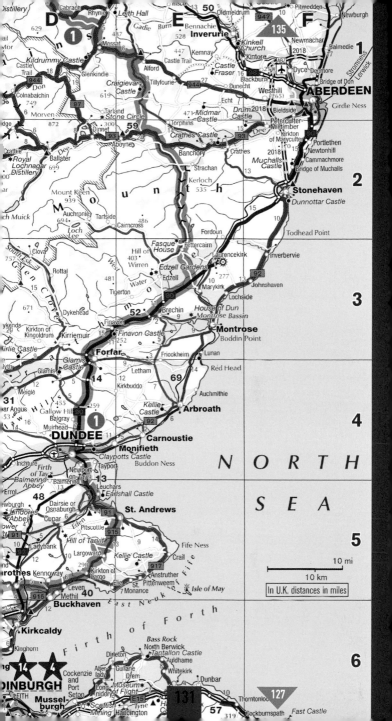

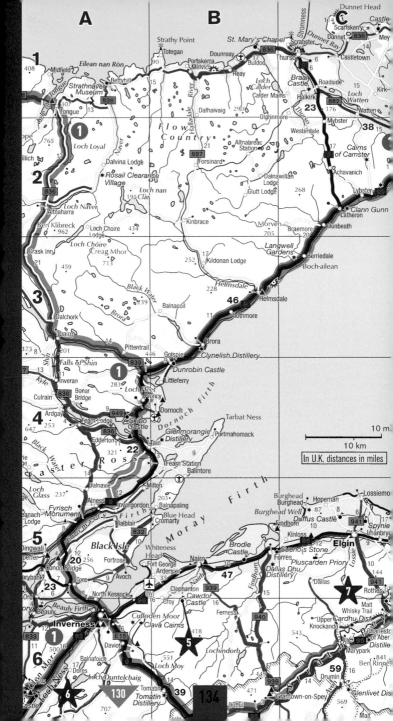

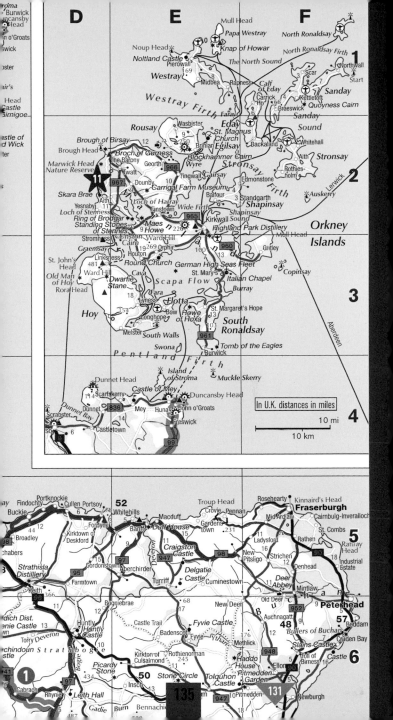

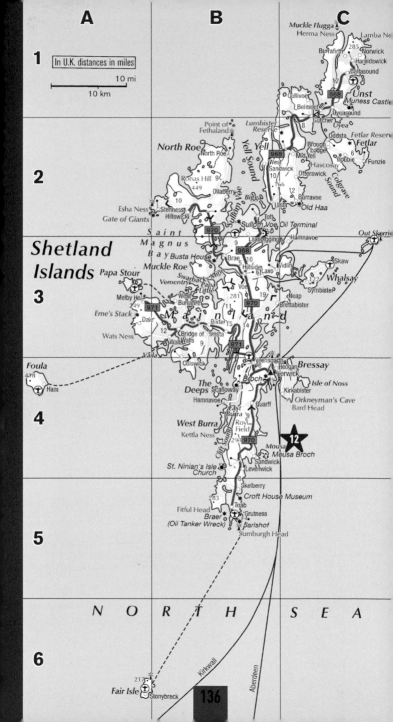

A **1**

In U.K. distances in miles

10 mi

10 km

B

Muckle Flugga
Herma Ness
Burrafirth   285   Norwick
Lamba Ne
Haroldswick
Baltasound
C

12
968   **Unst**
Gutcher   Muness Castle
Gullivoe   Uyeasound
Belmont   Uyea

Point of
Fethaland
North Roe
North Roe

Lumbister
Reserve

8   Oddsta   Fetlar Reserv
Brough   **Fetlar**
Lodge   6
Houbie   Funzie

North Roe   **Yell**   968   West   Mid Yell
Sandwick   Hascosay
Otterswick   **Colgrave**
Sound

2   Ronas Hill
449   Ollaberry   9
166   12   Burravoe
Bigga   Ulsta   *Old Haa*

10

Esha Ness   Stenness   Voe
Hillswick   Toft
Gate of Giants   Sullom Voe   Oil Terminal

Shetland   S a i n t   Laxo   Igbigging   Hamnavoe   Out Skerri

Islands   M a g n u s   968   Hiltside   Laxo
B a y   Brae   5   Widlin
Papa Stour   Busta House   Hamnavoe   Skaw
Muckle Roe   Swarbacks Minn   281   Voe   19   Neap   **Whalsay**
Vementry   Papa   Brettabister   Symbister

3   Melby Hol   West   Little   11   970
249   971   Burrafirth   14
Erne's Stack   Dale   M   a   i   n   l   a   n   d
Wats Ness   12   Bridge of   Tresta
Walls   Walls   9   971
Vaila   971
Culswick   Veensgarth
Foula   Ham   The   Scalloway   Broch   **Bressay**
478   Deeps   Lerwick
Hamnavoe   *Isle of Noss*
4   *West Burra*   East   Quarff   Kirkabister
Burra   Royl   *Orkneyman's Cave*
Field   Bard Head
Kettla Ness   294   970
St. Ninian's Isle   Mousa   ★ **12**
Church   Sandwick   Mousa Broch
Levenwick

8   Skelberry   *Croft House Museum*
Fitful Head   383   Toab
Braer   Grutness
(Oil Tanker Wreck)   *Jarlshof*
5   Sumburgh Head

N O R T H   S E A

6   217
Fair Isle   Stonybreck   Kirkwall   **136**   Aberdeen

DUNDAS

Glasgow

D Sq.

Barratt Trading Est

E

F

1

Swimming Pool

Corn St.

W. City

Payne St.

16

17

Craighall Rd.

Road

Dobbie's

Canal St.

Stow City College

New City Road

Buccleuch La.

W. Graham St.

Maitland

Tyndrum Street

Milton Street

Kyle St.

Calgary St.

Copper St.

2

Scott St.

Dalhousie St.

Rose St.

Renfrew

McPhater St.

Port Dundas Road

Passport Office Glasgow

Kennedy

Cowcaddens

Theatre Royal

Caledonian University

Road

geoge

tintosh School

iehall St.

iehall Lane

McLellan Gall.

Street

Mungo

Sauchiehall St.

Pitt St.

Kelvin Gallery

The Pavilion

Caledonian University

Omnibus Station

Killermont St.

Royal Concert Hall

Necropolis

Bath Street

Buchanan Galleries

Bath St.

Cathedral Street

3

est

Police Station

Regent

Byrdswood

West Regent Lane

St.

College

University

Collins Gallery

lice us!

George

D West George Lane

Street

Queen Street Station

W. George Sq.

George

Montrose

St. Vincent Lane

Street

Douglas

Bothwell St.

Wellington

St. Vincent Pl.

City Chambers

Cochrane St.

4

Bothwell Lane

Nile St.

Royal Ex. Sq.

Hutchesons Hall

Merchant

on Cadogan

Wellington Lane

Gordon St.

Renfield

Gallery Modern

Sheriff Court

City

Waterloo

Street

Mitchell St.

Buchanan

Queen St.

Brunswick St.

City Hall

St.

Holm St.

Hope

Virginia St.

Wilson

Bell St.

Brown St.

York St.

Argyle St.

Central Station

Union St.

Jamaica St.

Miller

Argyle St.

Argyle St.

Trongate

Albion St.

King St.

Broomielaw

Robertson St.

Oswald St.

Howard Street

Osborne St.

Tron Theatre

Clyde Place

Georges

Bridge St.

Glasgow Bridge

University

Fox St.

Howard St.

Stockwell

Pl.

Bridgegate

Saltmarket

Steel

5

ON

Clyde Place

Clyde

Bridge

St. Andrews Cathedral

St.

Justiciary Buildings

Peoples Palace

d

Kingston St.

Carlton Place

Victoria Bridge

Sheriff Court

Adelphi St.

Crown

Albert Bridge

Glasgow Green

Glasgow City Council

Nelson St.

Oxford St.

Central Mosque

Florence Street Clinic

6

Tradeston

Commerce

Bridge St.

Norfolk St.

Tistle St.

Crown St.

Ballater

Street

Commerce

Cook Street

Works Tradeston Store

Coburg St.

Portland St.

Bedford St.

Old Pl.

KEY TO ROAD ATLAS

Autobahn mit Anschlussstellen Motorway with junctions	
Autobahn in Bau Motorway under construction	
Mautstelle Toll station	
Raststätte mit Übernachtung Roadside restaurant and hotel	
Raststätte Roadside restaurant	
Tankstelle Filling-station	
Autobahnähnliche Schnellstraße mit Anschlussstelle Dual carriage-way with motorway characteristics with junction	
Fernverkehrsstraße Trunk road	
Durchgangsstraße Thoroughfare	
Wichtige Hauptstraße Important main road	
Hauptstraße Main road	
Nebenstraße Secondary road	
Eisenbahn Railway	
Autozug-Terminal Car-loading terminal	
Zahnradbahn Mountain railway	
Kabinenschwebebahn Aerial cableway	
Eisenbahnfähre Railway ferry	
Autofähre Car ferry	
Schifffahrtslinie Shipping route	
Landschaftlich besonders schöne Strecke Route with beautiful scenery	
Alleenstr. Touristenstraße Tourist route	
XI-V Wintersperre Closure in winter	
Straße für Kfz gesperrt Road closed to motor traffic	
8% Bedeutende Steigungen Important gradients	
Für Wohnwagen nicht empfehlenswert Not recommended for caravans	
Für Wohnwagen gesperrt Closed for caravans	
☀ Besonders schöner Ausblick Important panoramic view	

✳ *Wartenstein* ✳ *Umbalfälle*	Sehenswert: Kultur - Natur Of interest: culture - nature
	Badestrand Bathing beach
	Nationalpark, Naturpark National park, nature park
	Sperrgebiet Prohibited area
	Kirche Church
	Kloster Monastery
	Schloss, Burg Palace, castle
	Moschee Mosque
	Ruinen Ruins
	Leuchtturm Lighthouse
	Turm Tower
	Höhle Cave
	Ausgrabungsstätte Archaeological excavation
▲	Jugendherberge Youth hostel
♠	Allein stehendes Hotel Isolated hotel
⌂	Berghütte Refuge
▲	Campingplatz Camping site
✈	Flughafen Airport
✈	Regionalflughafen Regional airport
✈	Flugplatz Airfield
	Staatsgrenze National boundary
	Verwaltungsgrenze Administrative boundary
⊖	Grenzkontrollstelle Check-point
⊖	Grenzkontrollstelle mit Beschränkung Check-point with restrictions
ROMA	Hauptstadt Capital
VENEZIA	Verwaltungssitz Seat of the administration
	MARCO POLO Erlebnistour 1 MARCO POLO Discovery Tour 1
	MARCO POLO Erlebnistouren MARCO POLO Discovery Tours
★	MARCO POLO Highlight MARCO POLO Highlight

FOR YOUR NEXT TRIP...

MARCO POLO TRAVEL GUIDES

Travel with
Insider
Tips

INDEX

This index lists all sights, museums and destinations, plus the names of important people and key words featured in this guide. Numbers in bold indicate a main entry.

WRITE TO US

e-mail: info@marcopologuides.co.uk
Did you have a great holiday?
Is there something on your mind?
Whatever it is, let us know!
Whether you want to praise, alert us
to errors or give us a personal tip –
MARCO POLO would be pleased to
hear from you.
We do everything we can to provide the
very latest information for your trip.

Nevertheless, despite all of our authors'
thorough research, errors can creep in.
MARCO POLO does not accept any
liability for this. Please contact us by
e-mail or post.
MARCO POLO Travel Publishing Ltd
Pinewood, Chineham Business Park
Crockford Lane, Chineham
Basingstoke, Hampshire RG24 8AL
United Kingdom

PICTURE CREDITS
Cover Photograph: Cairngorms National Park, Ruins of Ruthven Barracks (Schapowalow: S. Spila)
Photos: BTCV (19 bottom); Corbis/Scottish Viewpoint Picture Library (58); DuMont Bildarchiv: Mosler (31, 93, 111); Gettyimages: N. Bidgood (18 top), marcoisler (68/69), J. Mitchell (18 centre), M. Runnacles (22); Gettyimages/AWL Images: J. WarburtonLee (110/111); Gettyimages/Universal Images Group: myLoupe (66); huberimages: O. Fantuz (5, 76/77, 84, 94/95), A. Stewart (78); Hud yer Wheesht: Erin McElhinney (18 bottom); H. Krinilz (flap right, 4 bottom, 8, 9, 15, 16/17, 20/21, 24, 29, 34, 36, 39, 57, 65, 73, 74/75, 75, 81, 83, 86/87, 88, 90, 104, 110, 112, 112/113, 114 top, 114 bottom, 115, 120, 126/127); laif: A. Artz (28 right), C. Boisvieux (30/31), K.H. Raach (51, 71), D. Schwelle (2, 7, 44, 49), laif/hemis.fr: G. Gerault (74); laif/Le Figaro Magazine: Rogery (30); laif/robertharding: J. Emmerson (40); Look/age fotostock (42/43); mauritius images/Alamy (flap left, 10), J. Bracegirdle (106/107), R. Clarkson (6), T. Gainey (26/27), P. Marshall (113), D. Pearson (11), S. Price (62); mauritius images/ANP Photo (12/13, 60/61); mauritius images/Foodanddrinkphotos (28 left); mauritius images/imagebroker: O. Schubert (109); mauritius images/Loop Images (99); mauritius images/Paul Stewart Editorial/Alamy (54); mauritius images/Robert Harding (4 top, 32/33); mauritius images/View Pictures (46, 52); mauritius images/Westend61 (3); Schapowalow: S. Spila (1); Scotland by Camper Ltd: David Campbell (19 top)

2nd edition 2019, fully revised and updated
Worldwide Distribution: Marco Polo Travel Publishing Ltd, Pinewood, Chineham Business Park, Crockford Lane, Basingstoke, Hampshire RG24 8AL, United Kingdom. E-mail: sales@marcopolouk.com
© MAIRDUMONT GmbH & Co. KG, Ostfildern
Chief editor: Stefanie Penck
Author: Martin Müller; editor: Jens Bey
Programme supervision: Lucas Forst-Gill, Susanne Heimburger, Johanna Jiranek, Nikolai Michaelis, Kristin Wittemann, Tim Wohlbold; picture editors: Gabriele Forst, Stefanie Wiese; What's hot: Martin Müller; wunder media, München
Cartography road atlas & pull-out map: © MAIRDUMONT, Ostfildern
Cover design, p. 1; design pull-out map: Karl Anders – Büro für Visual Stories, Hamburg; design inside: milchhof:atelier, Berlin; desgin p. 2/3, Discovery Tours: Susan Chaaban Dipl.Des. (FH)
Translated from German by Birgitt Lederer and Suzanne Kirkbright
Editorial office: SAW Communications, Redaktionsbüro Dr. Sabine A. Werner, Mainz: Julia Gilcher, Kristin Smolinna, Cosima Talhouni, Dr. Sabine A. Werner; prepress: SAW Communications, Mainz, in cooperation with alles mit Medien, Mainz

MIX
Paper from
responsible sources
FSC® C124385

DOS & DON'TS 👆

The Scots are neither stingy nor English

DON'T STOP ILLEGALLY

Scotland's landscape makes it tempting for campers to park the car and camp wherever there is a scenic view. The lay-bys on single track roads can be especially inviting, these are not suitable sites to overnight and you'll be endangering both yourself and traffic if you do. The same goes for camping at picnic spots: look out for signs prohibiting camping.

DON'T WAIT FOR YOUR BEER IN THE BAR

If you expect to be waited on and have your beer served at your table you could wait forever. In Scotland you have to order your beer at the bar counter and wait to collect it (and pay for it) there.

DO COME PROPERLY EQUIPPED

Time and again rangers have to rescue reckless tourists from Scotland's national parks and mountain regions. The weather can take a turn for the worse very quickly you should only go hiking or mountain climbing with the appropriate clothing and equipment.

DON'T FISH WITHOUT A LICENSE

Don't let the isolation deceive you, fishing without a license can turn out to be a costly mistake. Most of the rivers and lochs are on private property and require a fishing licence. Ignore the rules and you could be faced with a hefty fine!

DO REMEMBER THE MOSQUITO REPELLENT

Mosquito season is from May to June when these small irritating insects are drawn to water and invade the coastlines in their thousands. Without the proper protection camping and hiking can be a disaster but fortunately all good chemists sell insect repellent.

DON'T CALL THE SCOTS ENGLISH

Not only is this impolite but also incorrect. The Scots are independent and have had their own parliament since 1999. Given Scotland's turbulent history, every Scot will feel offended if you call them English.

DON'T BELIEVE THE CLICHÉ

To this day the Scots are still considered to be stingy yet you would be hard pressed to find a more hospitable nation or one that donates more to worthy causes.

DO GIVE THE FOOD A CHANCE

Fish & chips and nothing more? Wrong! Scotland is no longer a culinary wasteland and now boasts excellent gourmet restaurants. However, they do come at a price so you should make provision for them in your travel budget.